Afghanistan Returns

To

Brutal Past

Events Generally Unfolded As Perceived

By The Same Author ....

1. India's National Security
2. Military Governance in Pakistan
3. Menace of Maoist Insurgency in India
4. Rohingya Crisis
5. Balakot Air Strike
6. Jeene Ki Rah : Sukhi Jeevan Ki Kunji
7. A Quest For Happiness
8. A Man Who Saw God
9. A Quest For Self Enlightment
10. Essence of A Spritiual Quest
11. China's Global Strategy : A Potent Threat To Sovereignty of India

Afghanistan Returns
To
Brutal Past

Events Generally Unfolded As Perceived

Brig. R.A. Singh, VSM (Retd.)

Raj Publications
New Delhi - 110002

Afghanistan Returns To Brutal Past: Events Generally Unfolded As Perceived

First Published in 2022

ISBN 978-93-92066-00-9

₹ 450

Published by : **Raj Publications**
108, 4855/24 Ansari Road,
Daryaganj, New Delhi - 110002
Tel. : 09811010939
E-Mail: rajpublications@yahoo.co.in

Laser Typesetting : Aarati Computers, Delhi-110 009

Printed at : Balaji Offset, Delhi

Contents

Preface 9

1. Afghanistan "The Graveyard of Empires" 13
2. Emergence of Talibans 17
3. China's Despondency on US troops Withdrawal from Afghanistan 22
4. US Troops Withdrawal Precipitates Pak Dilemma in Afghanistan 26
5. US Forces Pull Out Affects China's Strategic Calculus in Afghanistan 31
6. Simmering Turmoil in Afghanistan Creates Dilemma for US Troops Withdrawal 36
7. Afghanistan Calling 40
8. Demography of Afghanistan Also Adds Fuel to The Fire 43
9. The Surge In Militias is A Recipe For Disaster 47
10. Taliban Surge in Afghanistan Gives Insomnia to Neighbours 51
11. Resurgence of Taliban Pushes India to Sidelines 55

12. China's Despondency May Aggravate Situation faster in Afghanistan 60

13. US Troops Withdrawal from Iraq-Another Scenario in Offing 64

14. Fall of Kabul Looks Imminent-US Too To Blame 68

15. Islamic Emirate of Afghanistan-'Not Yet Recognised' 72

16. Taliban Returns to Afghanistan 76

17. How Long Can Panjshir Resist Taliban Onlaught? 81

18. Afghanistan Likely to Be The Epicenter of Terrorism 84

19. China's Game Plan in Afghanistan After Taliban Take over 89

20. India's Strategic Options in Afghanistan after Taliban's Take over 93

21. How Potent is Al-Qaeda Threat By Al Qaeda To Kashmir? 97

22. Despondecy Looms Large over New Taliban Government in Afghanistan 102

23. Will Taliban bring 'Achhe Din' for Pakistan? 107

24. Likely Hurdles in Taliban's Governance of Afghanistan 110

25. Is Panjshir Still Resuscitating in Afghanistan? 115

26. Dilemma of Taliban in formation of New Government in Afghanistan 120

Index 124

Preface

Since the day, US announced withdrawal of NATO forces from Afghanistan, the events took a serious turn and happened so quickly, which surprised the entire world. I, as my passion, also started following and recording these happenings in shape of articles, sequencially as the events unfolded. Though my these notes are already in circulation, yet for the benifit of those readers who may have missed, I am putting these together as the text of this book on Afghanistan.

The sequence of events that unfolded in Afghanistan over recent months has surprised all the important players directly involved with the last 20 years war in the country, a historical Battlefield where the great game has been played for a long time. All political pundits had predicted that the previous government with 3.5 lacs US trained security troops would be able to re pulse Taliban invasion of cities. They were all proved wrong. Kabul had surrendered without resistance on August 15, the moment the armed groups arrived at its doors. The war torn country has not seen a durable government in the last four decades. From the 1979 invasion of Afghanistan by the former Soviet union to the recent exit of Western forces, none of the elected or appointed heads of state and government have succeeded in establishing a stable system. The soviets had installed governments of leftist parties while the US had introduced western democracy model, but all these experiments failed to make inroads into and Afghan society driven buy tribal system of strict rules and codes of life. The lack of tribal loyalty to US backed Ashraf Ghani government had been one of the reasons for his fall.

Following the effective collapse of the Islamic Republic of Afghanistan during the 2021 Taliban offensive, the Taliban declared the country an Islamic Emirate. A new caretaker government was announced on 7 September. As of 8 September 2021, no other country had formally recognized the Islamic Emirate of Afghanistan as the de jure government of Afghanistan.

Taliban has managed a walk over in Afghanistan as latter's army shamefully gave up resistance for the fear of reprisal. Unfortunately some leading regional powers are obscenely courting the blight of Taliban, which is reimposing a repressive, regressive, Islamist Dogma on Afghanistan. It hasn't taken very long for the unbridled bigotry of Taliban to embolden other Islamists extremists in Afghanistan and beyond.

On 2nd July 21 at 3:00 a.m. the US stealthily abandoned bagram airfield its largest facility in Afghanistan. The very unpleasantness of this singular act boosted the Talibans morale which would be etched in Afghans memory more than the cumulative errors of the US foreign policy over the last two decades. It was an equally bad omen for regional allies such as India.

With the relentless surge of the Taliban towards Kabul, in a complete mockery of the so called Doha Peace Accord, there was growing palpitation in neighbouring Islamabad Tehran, Tashkent, Beijing i Delhi and of course Moscow, each for their own specific reasons.

It was very painful and unpleasant to be abondoned

and that was just what the United States of America had done to Afghanistan and done so for the second time. Integral to this act of abandonment it was the the selfishness of not caring about those abandoned.

New Taliban interim government drawn exclusively from loyalist ranks formally begin work with the established hardliners in all the key positions with much grinding of teeth by the international community for the terrorists called extremists seizing reign of power in Kabul. Couple of foreign countries greeted the makeup of the new government in Afghanistan with caution and dismay after Taliban appointed hardliners veterans figures to top positions.

The Taliban, or "students" in the Pashto language, emerged in the early 1990s in northern Pakistan following the withdrawal of Soviet troops from Afghanistan. It is believed that the predominantly Pashtun movement first appeared in religious seminaries - mostly paid for by money from Saudi Arabia - which preached a hardline form of Sunni Islam. The promise made by the Taliban in Pashtun areas straddling Pakistan and Afghanistan was to restore peace and security and enforce their own austere version of Sharia, or Islamic law, once in power.

Pakistan's army Inter-Services Intelligence Directorate (ISI) has backed the Taliban since the group's origin in the mid-1990s. Under intense pressure in September 2001, the ISI briefly removed its experts and assistance, creating the same panic and flight to the Taliban that the U.S. withdrawal just did to the Afghan army. But the ISI quickly renewed its support and that aid continues today. The Taliban/ISI victory in Afghanistan will have significant consequences for Pakistan, some of which may be dangerous and violent.

Pakistan would continue to ride its most effective and time-tested strategies against India using an array of militant groups has proxies to continue bleed India. These groups that were operating in Afghanistan are now free to be used against India in Kashmir. The hope Pakistan has with Taliban coming to power is to intensify trouble in Kashmir with the help of Haqqani and other terrorist groups which is also not very easy since the armed forces of India are fully Geared to meet all these eventualities.

Pakistan which celebrated Taliban takeover of Afghanistan is now waking up to the realisation that the group's victory is inciting terrorist into insurgency in its own region, according to media reports. When Pakistan prime minister Imran Khan uplauded the Taliban victory and said that they broke "shackles of slavery" he was unaware that the outfits victory in a neighbouring country can trigger militants in his own country too.

The debate about whether India should engage with Taliban discreetly or in the open has shifted to whether India should recognise the Talibans. There is a widespread feeling that India Once again backed the wrong horse or at least didn't do course correction and engage the Taliban sufficiently in advance to protect its interests. Some even recommend that India should recognise Taliban and be pragmatic since India is on week ground and has very few options.

China is punting substantially on the return of the Taliban in Afghanistan with a high risk high return approach. While scenes of retreating US troops from Afghanistan may provide optical rhetorical and political fodder to the Chinese to claim one upmanship in the stressed US-China equation, it also brings the extremist Taliban in direct control of 91 kilometre land border between Afghanistan and China at the Wakhan corridor. Hard-nosed Chinese would recognise the practical risk involved in betting on the Taliban, but the pontential $1 trillion worth the world's largest lithium reserve in Afghanistan may make the risk worth a try.

Russia's Afghanistan failures in 1980s are driving the Kremlin's thinking of how to deal with the Taliban and possible rise of religious extremism near irs border. New large scale deployment to neighbouring states, Uzbekistan, Kyrgyzstan, Tajikistan and Turkmenistan or Afghanistan would be too much for the Russian armed forces. Russia has also deployed troops in large numbers to Syria, arrayed close to Ukraine and are now moving to Arctic to protect Russia's interests along the Northern Sea Route. Russia fears that a new refugee crisis would send more Islamist extremists back to Russia itself. Russia is calling on Central Asia countries not to allow Afghan refugee crossings that could eventually reach its borders. Though those Nations have closed their borders but borders are mostly porous. Russia maintains airbases in Kyrgyzstan and Tajikistan but has little other military presence. China has small base in Tajikistan as well, close to Afghan border. Other regional powers watching events in Kabul are Pakistan and India, as well as China, all with differing interests in the outcome.

Afghanistan is a notoriously difficult country to govern. Empire after empire, nation after nation have failed to pacify what is today the modern territory of Afghanistan, giving the region the nickname "Graveyard of Empires," even if sometimes those empires won some initial battles and made inroads into the region.

Seeing the happenings in Afghanistan and in the region I as an ex- service man could not resist, and had a look into the events that were fast un- folding and recorded the happenings, now to present it to the reader in shape of a book.

I have generally abstained from passing any opinion or judgement on various events unless it was absolutely inescapable to complete the text. The narrative itself projects the story and future courses of action and I feel there is no need to sway the readers one side of the other.

I shall be failing if I do not mention about my wife Rama who has always been a source of inspiration for me and has indirectly contributed a lot in production of this book without which I would have taken quite some time to complete the job.

- Brig R.A. Singh, VSM(Retd.)

1

Afghanistan "Graveyard of Empires"

Afghanistan is a notoriously difficult country to govern. Empire after empire, nation after nation have failed to pacify what is today the modern territory of Afghanistan, giving the region the nickname "Graveyard of Empires," even if sometimes those empires won some initial battles and made inroads into the region.

Afghanistan (meaning "land of the Afghans" or "Afghan land") has been a strategically important location throughout history. The land served as "a gateway to India, impinging on the ancient Silk Road, which carried trade from the Mediterranean to China". Sitting on many trade and migration routes, Afghanistan may be called the 'Central Asian roundabout' since routes converge from the Middle East, from the Indus Valley through the passes over the Hindu Kush, from the Far East via the Tarim Basin, and from the adjacent Eurasian Steppe.

From the Middle Ages to around 1750 the eastern part of Afghanistan was recognized as being a part of India while its western parts parts were included in Khorasan. Two of the four main capitals of Khorasan (Balkh and Herat) are now located in Afghanistan.

Islamic Emirate of Afghanistan, is a landlocked country at the crossroads of Central and South Asia. It is bordered by Pakistan to the east and south, Iran to the west, Turkmenistan and Uzbekistan to the north, and Tajikistan and China to the northeast. Occupying 652,864 square kilometers (252,072 sq mi), the country is predominately mountainous with plains in the north and the southwest that are separated by the Hindu Kush mountains. It is inhabited by 31.4 million people as of 2020, composed mostly of ethnic Pashtuns, Tajiks, Hazaras, and Uzbeks. Kabul serves as its capital and largest city.

Because of the frequency of invasion and the prevalence of tribalism in the area, its lawlessness lead to a situation where almost every village or house was built like a fortress, or qalat. Third, the physical terrain of Afghanistan makes conquest and rule extremely difficult, exacerbating its tribal tendencies. Afghanistan is dominated by some of the highest and more jagged mountains in the world. These include the Hindu Kush, which dominates the country and run through the center and south of the country, as well as the Pamir mountains in the east. The Pamir Knot — where the Hindu Kush, Pamir, Tian Shan, Kunlun, and Himalayas all meet is situated in Badakhshan in northeast Afghanistan.

Afghanistan is located on the main land route between Iran, Central Asia, and India, it has been invaded many times and settled by a plethora of tribes, many mutually hostile to each other and outsiders.

About the fierce Pashtuns, no less than Alexander the Great had said, as early as the fourth century BC: 'May God keep you away from the venom of the cobra, the teeth of the tiger, and the revenge of the Afghans'. However, within the comity of warlike Pashtuns, the 'martial' instincts of the Afridis from Tirah valley, is legendary. Controlling the gateway of Khyber Pass, Mughal Emperor Babar tried subduing their irascible behaviour, but the implacably hostile Afridis defied repeated attempts, even by subsequent armies of Mughal Emperors like Akbar, Jahangir, and Aurangzeb.

Michni Point, Pakistan's last outpost at the western end of the barren, winding Khyber Pass, stands sentinel over Torkham Gate, the deceptively orderly border crossing into Afghanistan. Frontier Scouts in gray shalwar kameezes (traditional tunics and loose pants) and black berets patrol the lonely station commanded by a major of the legendary Khyber Rifles, the militia force that has been guarding the border with Afghanistan since the nineteenth century, first for British India and then for Pakistan. This spot, perhaps more than any other, has witnessed the traverse of the world's great armies on campaigns of conquest to and from South and Central Asia. All eventually ran into trouble in their encounters with the unruly Afghan tribals.

Alexander the Great sent his supply trains through the Khyber, then skirted northward with his army to the Konar Valley on his campaign in 327 BC. There he ran into fierce resistance and, struck by an Afghan archer's arrow, barely made it to the Indus River with his life. Genghis Khan and the great Mughal emperors began passing through the Khyber a millennium later and ultimately established the greatest of empires—but only after reaching painful accommodations with the tribals.

Numbers of 300,000 trained and well-equipped Afghan soldiers, up against a ragtag militia of 75,000-odd Talibanis, are bandied with the additional element of considerable airpower at the Afghan Military's disposal. To rub in the humiliation, even the essentially clueless Joe Biden commented: "The Afghan military gave up, sometimes without trying to fight." While the bleak commentary on Afghan troops is true, however, the spin doctors in Washington DC have successfully managed to deflect the much-needed criticism of the performance of the world's most powerful military against a motley militia — despite the $2 trillion bill, nearly 2500 American soldiers returning in body bags, and the unprecedented access to all forms of military wherewithal, air cover and unanswerable military conduct. When the din and dust on Afghanistan under the Taliban does settle, serious questions on the performance and psyche of the American soldier will be awkwardly unavoidable and embarrassing, just as it has been so for the Afghan Army soldier.

When President Joe Biden addressed the chaotic scenes unfolding in Afghanistan in advance of the looming final retreat of U.S. forces, he said that no amount of military force could have delivered a different outcome in a country "known in history as the graveyard of empires."

The term evokes images—which have been immortalized on canvas and film — of colonial forces limping home, as indeed they have. However, critics say that it oversimplifies the country's history and the external political considerations that led to the retreats of the British, Soviets and Americans.

2

Emergence of Taliban

The Taliban, or "students" in the Pashto language, emerged in the early 1990s in northern Pakistan following the withdrawal of Soviet troops from Afghanistan. It is believed that the predominantly Pashtun movement first appeared in religious seminaries - mostly paid for by money from Saudi Arabia - which preached a hardline form of Sunni Islam.The promise made by the Taliban - in Pashtun areas straddling Pakistan and Afghanistan - was to restore peace and security and enforce their own austere version of Sharia, or Islamic law, once in power.

From south-western Afghanistan, the Taliban quickly extended their influence. In September 1995 they captured the province of Herat, bordering Iran, and exactly one year later they captured the Afghan capital, Kabul, overthrowing the regime of President Burhanuddin Rabbani - one of the founding fathers of the Afghan mujahideen that resisted the Soviet occupation. By 1998, the Taliban were in control of almost 90% of Afghanistan.

Afghans, weary of the mujahideen's excesses and infighting after the Soviets were driven out, generally welcomed the Taliban when they first appeared on the scene. Their early popularity was largely due to their success in stamping out corruption, curbing lawlessness and making the roads and the areas under their control safe for commerce to flourish. But the Taliban also introduced or supported punishments in line with their strict interpretation of Sharia law - such as public executions of convicted murderers and adulterers, and amputations for those found guilty of theft. Men were required to grow beards and women had to wear the all-covering burka. The Taliban also banned television, music and cinema, and disapproved of girls aged 10 and over going to school. They were accused of various human rights and cultural abuses. One notorious example was in 2001, when the Taliban went ahead with the destruction of the famous Bamiyan Buddha statues in central Afghanistan, despite international outrage.

Pakistan has repeatedly denied that it was the architect of the Taliban enterprise, but there is little doubt that many Afghans who initially joined the movement were educated in madrassas (religious schools) in Pakistan. Pakistan was also one of only three countries, along with Saudi Arabia and the United Arab Emirates (UAE), which recognised the Taliban when they were in power in Afghanistan. It was also the last country to break diplomatic ties with the group.At one point, the Taliban threatened to destabilise Pakistan from areas they controlled in the north-west. One of the most high-profile and internationally condemned of all Pakistani Taliban attacks took place in October 2012, when schoolgirl Malala Yousafzai was shot on her way home in the town of Mingora. A major military offensive two years later following the Peshawar school massacre greatly reduced the group's influence in Pakistan though. At least three key figures of the Pakistani Taliban had been killed in US drone strikes in 2013, including the group's leader, Hakimullah Mehsud.

Many senior Taliban leaders reportedly took refuge in the Pakistani city of Quetta, from where they guided the Taliban. But the existence of what was dubbed the "Quetta Shura" was denied by Islamabad.Despite ever higher numbers of foreign troops, the Taliban gradually regained and then extended their influence in Afghanistan, rendering vast tracts of the country insecure, and violence in the country returned to levels not seen since 2001.

Pakistan's army Inter-Services Intelligence Directorate (ISI) has backed the Taliban since the group's origin in the mid-1990s. Under intense pressure in September 2001, the ISI briefly removed its experts and assistance, creating the same panic and flight to the Taliban that the U.S. withdrawal just did to the Afghan army. But the ISI quickly renewed its support and that aid continues today. The Taliban/ISI victory in Afghanistan will have significant consequences for Pakistan, some of which may be dangerous and violent.

Mullah Omar, the founder of the Taliban, was trained by the ISI during the war against the Soviets in the 1980s. When he was wounded, he got medical attention in a Pakistani hospital. After the Soviets retreated out of Afghanistan, he was one of many warlords fighting for control of the country. As he created the Taliban, the Pakistani army gave him support for the drive on Kabul in 1996 that gave the Taliban control of most of the country. Pakistan provided experts and advisers for the Taliban military, oil for its economy and was their supply route to the outside world.

The Taliban is inherently an inflexible, dogmatic and puritanical phenomenon that vehemently disallows exceptions, leniencies and accommodations. For anyone to genuinely believe that the Taliban in its new avatars will accede to their interests, is very unlike and immatured expectations.

The attention of the world was drawn to the Taliban in Afghanistan in the wake of the 11 September 2001 World

Trade Center attacks in New York. The Taliban were accused of providing a sanctuary for the prime suspects - Osama Bin Laden and his Al-Qaeda movement. On October 7, 2001, a US-led military coalition launched attacks in Afghanistan, and by the first week of December the Taliban regime had collapsed. The group's then-leader, Mullah Mohammad Omar, and other senior figures, including Bin Laden, evaded capture despite one of the largest manhunts in the world.

Despite ever higher numbers of foreign troops, the Taliban gradually regained and then extended their influence in Afghanistan, rendering vast tracts of the country insecure, and violence in the country returned to levels not seen since 2001. Mullah Mansour was killed in a US drone strike in May 2016 and replaced by his deputy Maulawi Hibatullah Akhundzada, who remains in control of the group.

The most immediate international concern relates to the presence of terrorist networks in Afghanistan. The Taliban's political ascendance poses a huge counter terrorism challenge as globally-oriented terror groups such as al-Qaeda and ISIS could create a favorable environment in Taliban-led Afghanistan to step up their activities. While the Taliban had pledged to sever links with al-Qaeda as part of their now-discredited deal with the U.S. in February 2020, there is hardly any evidence of their willingness to honor their word and al-Qaeda has praised the Taliban for their victory.

A little more than a month after toppling the Western-backed government in Kabul, Afghanistan's new Taliban rulers are facing internal enemies who have adopted many of the tactics of urban warfare that marked their own successful guerrilla campaign

The Taliban have said repeatedly that they will not allow Afghanistan to be used as a base for attacks on other countries. But some Western analysts believe the return of the Islamist group to power has invigorated groups like

ISIS-K and al Qaeda, which had made Afghanistan their base when the Taliban last ruled the country.

ISIS-K is believed to draw many of its fighters from the ranks of the Taliban or the Pakistani version of the Taliban, known as the TTP, but much of the way it operates remains little understood.It has fought the Taliban over smuggling routes and other economic interests but it also supports a global Caliphate under Islamic law, in contrast with the Taliban which insists it has no interest in anywhere outside Afghanistan.

"Funding support to the Khorasan branch from the core is believed to have effectively dried up," the report said. However, the report said signs of divisions within the Taliban, which have already started to emerge, could encourage more fighters to defect as the wartime insurgency tries to reshape itself into a peacetime administration.It remains active and dangerous, particularly if it is able, by positioning itself as the sole pure rejectionist group in Afghanistan, to recruit disaffected Taliban and other militants to swell.

3

China's Despondency On US Troops Withdrawal from Afghanistan

The final phase of US war in Afghanistan mark the end with its troops withdrawal from 01 May. This day was set for the official withdrawal of the remaining forces about 2500 US and 7000 Nato soldiers. Though these troops are still vulnerable to attacks during pullout as Taliban has not said so.

In 2021, President Biden has inherited Donald Trump's decisions for complete withdrawal of US troops from Afghanistan and Somalia where, yet again, the "enemy" in the form of Taliban (and affiliates) and Al-Shabab, respectively, is waiting menacingly. Somalia withdrawal has already happened and the ravaged territory is again left precariously poised. Afghanistan as the hub of regional/ global terror has an altogether different portent at stake. Clearly the deadline for complete withdrawal of the troops by May 1, 2021, is staring in the face for the force of about 2,500 troops (down from 1,00,000 in 2011) and the conflated "peace agreement" with the Taliban that underwrites such a withdrawal, remains routinely and supremely violated. The surge of marauding Taliban towards an embattled Kabul continues and herein to assume that 2,500 US troops would be able to withstand pressures that a one-time composition of 1,00,000 could not — let alone the situation when even this miniscule element departs as planned — is disastrous.

China has historically tiptoed gingerly around Afghanistan by tacitly supporting the Afghan Mujahedeen in the Soviet-Afghan war owing to Beijing's own competitive rift with Moscow ~ though the subsequent experience of the rule in the 1990s would scar Beijing's outlook towards dispensations in Kabul, very counterintuitively, from the preferences of its 'all-weather friend' in Islamabad. Contrary to the expected hullabaloo of having American troops in its 'backyard', China would rather punt on Afghan 'stability' with American soldiers-on-ground, rather than hope for the same through a puritanical dispensation like the Taliban. The primary motivation for China to seek 'stability' in Kabul is premised on a moderate Afghan dispensation's ability to rein-in Chinese Islamist insurgents like Turkestan Islamic Party (TIP) or East Turkestan Islamic Movement (ETIM), which seek to establish an Islamic state of East Turkestan in China's contiguous Xinjiang province. These China-facing Islamist groups had been given active support, training and afforded bases by the Taliban- Al Qaida groups, prior to the disruption of that eco-system by the current pro-West Afghan dispensation, in conjunction with the American/NATO troops. So, while Pakistan continuously pinned its hope on 'strategic depth' in Afghanistan via the return of the Taliban, the Chinese would realistically not have the Taliban.

The hallmarks of this elusive approach were visible in Beijing's handling of Afghanistan, with which it shares a 76-kilometrelong land border. China's historical appreciation of Afghanistan as the 'graveyard of empires', has spared it the expansionist eye that governs, militarily or economically, all its other neighbours under the 'going out' stratagem. The singular aspiration that China harbours for Afghanistan is 'stability'; this breeds complicated, contradictory and unmentionable moves distinct from the usual Chinese tact, which warrants a constant hawk eye and subtle manipulations, but without getting dragged into the nowin swamp of Afghanistan.

The comparative delta of upsetting the applecart as it is cast now (as opposed to a Pakistan- supported Taliban government), is a net loss to Beijing. Despite covert assurances by Taliban leadership to Chinese mediators to not target its investments and assets, the Chinese know that the Taliban are not a monolithic, disciplined and trustworthy entity. The current faciliatory game of the Chinese is very tentative and they have not put their weight behind the Taliban, as done by the Pakistanis.

The Chinese would ideally seek a status-quo situation that keeps the moderate government in Kabul on perennial tenterhooks, desperate for more international investments (where it can outplay, 'outfund' and control Indian influence), but without risking having a lawless Taliban-like revisionist government. Even the CPEC (China Pakistan Economic Corridor) assets in Pakistan are susceptible to attacks from China's own Islamist insurgent groups, and while it can exert formal pressure on the Pakistani Military to squeeze them in Pakistan, the same may not be possible with a Taliban government in Kabul.

The Chinese have a very pessimistic outlook about the fate of ongoing US-Taliban peace talks. China remains convinced about the imminent rupture to the delicate equilibrium in Afghanistan right now and is sure that the return of the Taliban or even an indecisive civil war between rival factions is to the net detriment of Chinese interests. Beijing views the American urgency to 'pullout' troops from

Afghanistan as imprudent, as that is sure to lead to chaos and a bloodshed in the region, with vulnerable neighbours like China left to face consequences and spillovers. China is paranoid about religious radicalisation and violence on its side, especially given its ongoing purge against its own Uyghur populace. China picked on the possibilities of this awkward development early and shifted gears from 'calculated indifference' to 'strategic engagement'. China has since made strategic moves in Afghanistan in terms of mediation across the board, flaunting its ostensible 'neutrality'. It has opened talks with Taliban directly, facilitated joint dialogues (e.g. through Shanghai Cooperation Organization) as key participant, as also invested in building a military base in Badakhshan province, for the current Ashraf Ghani government. Last week in a curious development, the Afghan National Security Adviser, Hamdullah Mohib, met the Chinese special envoy for Afghanistan, Liu Jian, to discuss issues of 'cooperation on peace and security'! Clearly, the Chinese haven't forsaken the incumbent and beleaguered Ashraf Ghani government yet.

The Dragon is confused and persisting with engagement in the interim to salvage the situation in Afghanistan, betting that the incoming Biden dispensation does a rethink on the proposed 'pull-out', which will be inadvertently preferable to both Beijing and Delhi.

For once and uniquely so, the Chinese preference for a government in Afghanistan would be more aligned to the preferences of New Delhi, than to those of Islamabad.

Pursuing a unilateral role in the 'graveyard of empires' is a clear no-no, and Beijing's international credibility in mustering a multilateral force (beyond Pakistan, which has its own complicated angularities), would prove challenging.

4

US Troops Withdrawal Precipitates Pak Dilemma in Afghanistan

The announcement by President Joe Biden that the US will withdraw all its troops from Afghanistan by September 11, 2021, the 20th anniversary of the 9/11 attacks, has sent tremors through the region's fault-lines.

The Biden plan has no strings attached. There are about 2,500-3,500 US troops in Afghanistan at present, plus a NATO force of under 8,000. A co-ordinated withdrawal is expected to begin soon.

The impact of this announcement on various actors within Afghanistan and outside is bound to be far-reaching. It can be said with certainty that no country in the region will remain untouched.

This is a moment of both vindication and concern in Islamabad. The Taliban are a creation of the Pakistani security establishment. After the US invasion of Afghanistan, they removed themselves to safe havens in Pakistan territory, and the Taliban High Council operated from Quetta in Balochistan. It was Pakistan that persuaded the Taliban to do a deal with the Trump Administration. For the Pakistani Army, which has always seen Afghanistan in terms of "strategic depth" in its forever hostility with India, a Taliban capture of Afghanistan would finally bring a friendly force in power in Kabul after 20 years. India, which has had excellent relations with the Karzai and Ghani governments, would be cut to size.

But a US withdrawal also means Pakistan will need to shoulder the entire burden of the chaos that experts predict. Civil war is not ruled out and with it, the flow of refugees into Pakistan once again, even as the country struggles with refugees from the first Afghan war. All this at a time when the economy is flailing, and Pakistan stays afloat on an IMF loan with strict conditionalities. Plus, the Taliban are not a monolith, and have recently shown streaks of independence from Pakistan. It has to guard against instability in Afghanistan from spilling over the border. Pakistan's eastern front with India is quiet at the moment, so that is one headache less, but it would remain a concern for the Pakistan Army.

Overall, on terror, the Pakistani 'establishment' realises that it has bitten more than it can chew and needs to do major course correction. However, vested interests, political short-termism and rudderless leadership have ensured that the Pakistanis keep walking deep into the religious minefield and with a possible Taliban-run Afghanistan, it will be the worst self-goal and not the 'Strategic Depth', as once envisaged. Prime Minister Imran Khan repeatedly talks about Pakistan being 'the biggest victim of terror' — he does so unconvincingly with the full knowledge of how it all started, though he is statistically right about the Pakistani body count owing to terror, and with the inevitable Taliban-run Afghanistan looming, the terror numbers will spiral for Pakistan, before anywhere.

Biden's decision to pull out troops from Afghanistan

will also give an upper hand to regional players, which are vying for a bigger role in the country. Countries like Pakistan, India, China and Russia have their own strategic interests, which are better served without a US presence in Afghanistan.

Pakistani Foreign Minister Shah Mahmood Qureshi, who held talks with his German counterpart Heiko Maas in Berlin earlier this week, told DW that Islamabad will remain an important player in the Afghan peace process. "Pakistan will benefit from peace in Afghanistan. It will open the door to increased trade with Kabul, and many pending development projects can be completed," he said.

Taliban are a heterogeneous entity with explosive faultlines within, held together by their medieval and totalitarian outlook that has enough 'bind' when in opposition — but when entrusted with power, the collectiveness of Taliban is grossly suspected. Pakistan supports only specific elements within the Taliban and often plays one against the other. Looming nationalistic undercurrents of Pashtunistan which subliminally resonates on both sides of the Durand Lines that divides Pashtun families and clans, is vulnerable to eruption, should the current fixation with 'foreigners' (read, US/NATO troops) subside.

Only a 'dominant' position for the Taliban (like earlier, when it controlled 80 per cent land, and was fighting for the rest, unsuccessfully) is preferable to Pakistani interests, as opposed to the complete control of Afghanistan, by the Taliban — as then the distraction, reliance and 'sustenance lifeline' afforded by Pakistan/ISI for the Taliban to continue waging its internal wars, may not be required anymore! Pakistan hosts the lawless Pashtun swathes along the Af-Pak border, with over three million restive Afghan refugees on its soil. With no internal strife, the Taliban could train their focus on their Pashtun brethren and their perceived woes in Pakistan.

New Delhi, which was hoping to be part of the Blinken initiative, would be nervous about the US withdrawal. India was on the outer edges of the Trump drive to exit Afghanistan that culminated in the Doha Accord, and was a reluctant supporter of the "intra-Afghan talks" between the Taliban and Afghan government. When the Biden Administration came in, India was hopeful of a US reset. The Blinken proposal gave India a role, by recognising it as a regional stakeholder, but this proposal seems to have no future. The Haqqani group, fostered by the ISI, would have a large role in any Taliban regime. Another concern would be India-focused militants such as Laskhar- e-Toiba and Jaish-e-Mohamed, which the Indian security establishment already believes to have relocated in large numbers to Afghanistan.

"India has been the largest regional contributor to Afghan reconstruction, but New Delhi has not shown an inclination to pursue a deeper defense relationship with Kabul," said a recent report on Afghanistan by the Independent Congressional Research Service.

"Pakistan's security establishment, fearful of strategic encirclement by India, apparently continues to view the Afghan Taliban as a relatively friendly and reliably anti-India element in Afghanistan. India's diplomatic and commercial presence in Afghanistan and US rhetorical support for it exacerbates Pakistani fears of encirclement," said the CRS report.

China would have much to lose from instability in Afghanistan as this could have an impact on the China Pakistan Economic Corridor. A Taliban regime in Afghanistan might end up stirring unrest in the Xinjiang Autonomous region, home to the Uighur minority. Conversely, as an ally of Pakistan, it could see a bigger role for itself in Afghanistan.

The US exit is for Russia a full circle after its own defeat at the hands of US-backed Mujahideen and exit from Afghanistan three decades ago. In recent years, Russia has taken on the role of peacemaker in Afghanistan. But both the Taliban and the Afghan government have been wary of its efforts. After a conference in March of Russia, US, China and Pakistan, along with Taliban and Afghan delegates, a joint statement by the four principals said they did not support the establishment of an Islamic Emirate, leaving the Taliban angry. Russia's growing links with Pakistan could translate into a post-US role for Moscow in Afghanistan.

Yet Pakistan wants a strong role for the Taliban in future Afghan governance. Its regional interests are better served with a powerful Taliban presence in its western neighborhood. This, however, would not guarantee peace in Afghanistan.

5

US Forces Pull out Affects China's Strategic Calculus in Afghanistan

The U.S. withdrawal from Afghanistan could reshape dynamics across South and Central Asia, should Afghanistan take a turn for the worst as many fear. Developments are being watched closely in Beijing, which has increased its presence in the region under the Belt and Road Initiative, and continues to have concerns about the potential for terrorism to spill across international borders.

As a close neighbour of Afghanistan, China is a supporter, mediator, and facilitator of the Afghan peace process. Even more than other countries, China hopes to see Afghanistan rid itself of war, achieve peace, move toward stability, start reconstruction, and resume development. But for the moment, achieving peace in Afghanistan is a top priority, which is also the basis and prerequisite for its future development.

The progressively deteriorating security situation in Afghanistan, and the potential risks that it could pose to Beijing's long-term economic endeavours, is an unsettling prospect for China. However, the first and perhaps most compelling motivation for China in pursuing greater engagement with Afghanistan is its unease regarding the geographical proximity between Afghanistan, and its own Uighur Muslim-dominated Xinjiang Province. Afghanistan is home to the Taliban and a number of other transnational terrorist outfits, and the restive Xinjiang region is claimed by Chinese authorities to be the breeding ground for the "three evils" of terrorism, separatism and religious extremism, plaguing their country. Moreover, there exists the dangerous possibility of radical elements hailing from foreign lands, using Afghanistan as a launch pad to establish links with the already vulnerable Uighur-inhabited areas of China. There is also the fear that the ideological influence of pan-Islamic groups operating in the tribal areas of Pakistan and Afghanistan could spill over into China, exacerbating separatism in Xinjiang.

In recent years, China has been expanding its diplomatic and economic profile in Afghanistan, with its policy evolving from being premised on 'calculated indifference', to strategic engagement. Although China's actions may be predicated on domestic compulsions, Afghanistan could also benefit in the process, especially in relation to China's transcontinental connectivity ventures. Other considerations like China's geographical proximity to the war-weary country, a track record of refraining from intervening in the domestic affairs of the Afghans, and distinct strategic leverage over Pakistan, could be used by Beijing to help Afghanistan break out of the longstanding security quagmire. This brief explores the geo-strategic motivations behind growing Chinese engagement in Afghanistan, despite western opprobrium regarding the "free-loading" nature of the same.

Since 2010, China has increased its economic aid and

investment in Afghanistan, notably with announcement by Metallurgical Corporation of China (MCC) pledging $3.5 billion to develop Aynak Copper mines. China has since been mining copper outside of Kabul.

Crucially, Beijing's influence isn't restricted to the key players within Afghanistan. It is also the principal economic benefactor of both Pakistan and Iran, Afghanistan's two largest neighbours. China has been by far the biggest foreign investor in Pakistan for a while. And earlier this year, it announced a $400 million investment in Iran, while also continuing to purchase Tehran's oil despite US sanctions. That clout will prove useful in Afghanistan too.

Neither Islamabad nor Tehran can afford to upset Beijing, which can count on them to use their contacts and influence to put pressure on the Taliban and other militias to stay in line. In effect, China — unlike the Soviet Union in the 1980s and the US since 2001 — might not need a large physical presence in Afghanistan to wield similar influence because unlike those other powers, it isn't seen as the enemy by any major player in the country.

Now the dangerous snake pit created and abetted by the Pakistani "establishment" has managed to wear out the US/NATO troops, the sectarian and ethnic minorities in Afghanistan are left vulnerable. Pakistan has bequeathed its cancerous and manipulative approach onto the warlords and other terror groups operating in Afghanistan, and like its blood-soiled streets of Quetta — the augury of future Afghanistan for "minorities" (like in Pakistan) is dark and foreboding.

Taliban are a heterogeneous entity with explosive faultlines within, held together by their medieval and totalitarian outlook that has enough 'bind' when in opposition — but when entrusted with power, the collectiveness of Taliban is grossly suspected. Pakistan supports only specific elements within the Taliban and often plays one against the other. Looming nationalistic undercurrents of Pashtunistan which subliminally resonates on both sides of the Durand Lines that divides Pashtun families and clans, is vulnerable to eruption, should the current fixation with 'foreigners' (read, US/NATO troops) subside.

China seeks to leverage the fact that it doesn't have a history of invasion/war against Afghanistan, unlike other major actors like the US and Russia. Over the last five years China's engagement has significantly widened from being an indifferent economic player to extending cooperation in security, counter-terrorism, dealing with the challenges of the coronavirus and aiding Afghanistan's connectivity with theneighbouring states through BRI. Given the current realities, Beijing is likely to be the second most important foreign actor in Afghanistan (after Pakistan) owing to several facilitating factors. First, despite the economic slow-down post-Covid-19, Beijing seems to have a sufficient appetite to sustain investments catering to its strategic objectives; second, its all-weather friendship with Pakistan provides it ample space and comfort to operate in Afghanistan; third, Chinese presence in Afghanistan's neighbourhood, i.e. Central Asia, Iran, etc. is likely to facilitate its future engagement with Kabul; and fourth, China's readiness to offer military assistance through equipment, training, etc. is of appeal to Afghanistan, which aspires for military build-up.

China would have much to lose from instability in Afghanistan as this could have an impact on China Pakistan Economic Corridor. A Taliban regime in Afghanistan might end up stirring unrest in the Xinjiang Autonomous region, a home to the Uighur minority. Conversely as an ally of Pakistan, it could see a bigger role for itself in Afghanistan.

It's also a particularly worrying scenario for India,

which has for the most part steadfastly refused to engage in dialogue with the Taliban, a group that has long relied on financial and logistical support from Pakistan's military. But while the situation bears close similarities to Afghanistan 30 years ago, there's one key difference that could help or hurt New Delhi: the role of China.

6

Simmering Turmoil in Afghanistan Creates Dilemma for US Troops Withdrawal ?

Afghanistan is often known as the "Graveyard of Empires," because the foreign invaders who thought they would make great military advances all lost their battles in the mountains and deserts, confronted by the stubborn resistance of Afghan tribes.

Now, the American government's narrative of the war on terror failed, so American forces and their allies want to leave.

Surveys in the US showed that many people see it as a "lost war." In 20 years, more than 20,000 US soldiers and officers were wounded in Afghanistan, and 2,300 were killed.

It is quite symbolic for the Biden government to choose September 11 as the deadline for its withdrawal from Afghanistan, given its significance from the September 11, 2001 twin tower crash orchestrated by the Al-Qaeda, which shook America to its core. In a bid to destroy Al-Qaeda, under the guise of protecting local and global security, the US initiated the war in Afghanistan.

After the longest war (20 years) in US history with far more investments than what was spent to rebuild Europe after the Second World War ~ the same Taliban that was pushed out of Kabul in 2001 is waiting menacingly outside Kabul, to reoccupy the unforgiving war-torn lands. Pakistan had sown, nurtured and unleashed the fury of the Taliban to perpetuate its own ambitions of 'Strategic Depth' (not complete control, because Pakistan more than any other nation, understands the Afghan psyche and inevitabilities).

The announcement by President Joe Biden that the US will withdraw all its troops from Afghanistan by September 11, 2021, the 20th anniversary of the 9/11 attacks, has sent tremors through the region's fault-lines.

An alarming assessment from US and Western intelligence analysts say that Kabul could fall to Taliban in less than a year after full withdrawal of US Troops, slated to be completed by 11 Sep 21. According to reports from Afghanistan, Taliban are now in control of 50 out of 370 districts of the country. Recent Taliban videos reveal that in some case they are winning without even firing a shot. In light of this alarming situation, US is likely to consider slowing down of pace of withdrawal which could include keeping Bagram Air Base to allow US Military keep some control for emergency use. This is particularly so since Pak PM has expressed his apprehension that Pak would be targeted for revenge by terrorists again if agreed to host US based for operations against Afghanistan.

As for India ,it has a real challenge on its hands. So far India has stuck to supporting the government in Kabul, but with ground reality changing fast with Taliban ramping up fighting and capturing number of district since May. India has two Strategic objectives, first. it wants to prevent

Pak from using Afghanistan as strategic depth against India once Americans leave. A Taliban takeover of Afghanistan is likely to embolden Pak to use its Afghan proxies against India, with possible ramifications for Kashmir. Second. India has made substantial investments in Afghanistan, around $ 3 billion, that need to be protected. Since current geopolitics not favouring India's ties with Iran and Russia, it cannot bank multilateral approach to protect its Afghan interest. In this scenario talking to Taliban makes sense.

Despite strident public posturing, the Pakistani 'establishment' too has woken to the horrors of having a Taliban-run Afghanistan next door. Secondly, while historically the US grudgingly soft-peddled the notorious Pakistani 'duplicity' due to its selfish requirements of Pakistani supply routes to maintain its assets in Afghanistan ~ hereinafter it would no longer be necessary to pander to Pakistani whims, beyond a point.

Pakistan has already sounded the red herring on the 'security vacuum' in Afghanistan and added that it would not tolerate 'terrorist activities' in Afghanistan ~ even though, as the progenitor of the Taliban, it would know better. The so called 'peace-dialogue' with the Taliban that the Pakistanis had championed, is now stuttering and faltering, with the Talibanis gleefully reneging on their peace commitments.

Today, a more complete dominance by the Taliban looms with the impending pull-back of US troops. The Chinese will maintain 'hard-borders' given their own vulnerabilities with the Uighur uprising, and the pandemic-fatigued Iran will struggle to offer any meaningful opposition to the Taliban. Potentially, the Taliban could crush all opposition and become the 'export hub' of its puritanical-revisionist impulses, for which the first porous destination would be Pakistan.

But a US withdrawal also means Pakistan will need to

shoulder the entire burden of the chaos that experts predict. Civil war is not ruled out and with it, the flow of refugees into Pakistan once again, even as the country struggles with refugees from the first Afghan war. All this at a time when the economy is flailing, and Pakistan stays afloat on an IMF loan with strict conditionalities. Plus, the Taliban are not a monolith, and have recently shown streaks of independence from Pakistan. It has to guard against instability in Afghanistan from spilling over the border. Pakistan's eastern front with India is quiet at the moment, so that is one headache less, but it would remain a concern for the Pakistan Army.

Overall, on terror, the Pakistani 'establishment' realises that it has bitten more than it can chew and needs to do major course correction. However, vested interests, political short-termism and rudderless leadership have ensured that the Pakistanis keep walking deep into the religious minefield and with a possible Taliban-run Afghanistan, it will be the worst self-goal and not the 'Strategic Depth', as once envisaged.

After the full withdrawal of troops, Taliban are likely to see the war, which they believe they have already won, to its completion. The recently published US Threat Assessment Report, an annual US intelligence briefing, said prospects for a peace deal are dim, the Taliban are confident of victory in the battlefield, and the Afghan government will struggle to hold them at bay.

7

Afghanistan Calling

On 02 July 21, at 3 am, the US stealthily abondoned Bagram airfield, its largest facility in Afghanistan. The very unpleasantness of this singular act has boosted the Taliban's morale, which will be etched in Afghan memory more than the cumulative errors of the US foreign policy over the last two decades. It is an equally bad omen for regional allies such as India.

"Ever since the remaining U.S. troops began pulling out on May 1, the Taliban have made rapid territorial advances. If the Taliban had controlled 73 of Afghanistan's 407 districts before May 1, the number of districts went up to 157 in two months as of June 29, according to the Long War Journal. They contest another 151 districts, which leaves 79 districts firmly in the hands of the government. The Taliban's military offensive is focussed on the northern districts, far away from their southern strongholds, and several provincial capitals are under threat".

"Now, when the U.S. is leaving and the Taliban are advancing, Pakistan is again in the spotlight. A violent military takeover of Afghanistan by the Taliban may not serve Pakistan's core interests. Pakistan wants to check India's influence in Afghanistan and bring the Taliban to Kabul. But a violent takeover, like in the 1990s, would lack international acceptability, leaving Afghanistan unstable for a foreseeable future. In such a scenario, Pakistan could face another influx of refugees from Afghanistan and a strengthening of anti-Pakistan terror groups, such as the Tehrik-i-Taliban. From a strategic point of view, Pakistan would prefer the Taliban being accommodated in power through negotiations and a peaceful settlement, which would also allow Rawalpindi to stabilise its conflict-ridden western border. But it's not clear whether Pakistan has the capacity to shape the post-American outcome in Afghanistan.

Pakistan has long been based on the strategic depth concept, which implies establishing a puppet regime in Afghanistan to focus all resources and attention on the conflict with India. Today, there are no real signs of this foreign policy paradigm receiving Islamabad's rejection. Surprisingly, even despite the United States and NATO's efforts, Islamabad has not abandoned these strategies. Perhaps, in addition to Pakistan, the Taliban's rise to power is not beneficial in the region and beyond. Moreover, this scenario can be avoided by limiting Islamabad's support for the radical movement.

"So, there could be three scenarios, according to experts. One, there could be a political settlement in which the Taliban and the government agree to some power-sharing mechanism and jointly shape the future of Afghanistan. As of now, this looks like a remote possibility. Two, an all-out civil war may be possible, in which the government, economically backed and militarily trained by the West, holds on to its positions in key cities and the Taliban expand its reach in the countryside, while other ethnic militias fight for their fiefs. This is already unfolding. A third scenario would be of the Taliban taking over the country."

"New Delhi has not denied reports of its outreach to the Taliban. This signals a late but realist acknowledgement from the Indian side that the Taliban would play a critical role in Afghanistan in the coming years. India has three critical areas in dealing with the Taliban. One, protecting its investments, which run into billions of rupees, in Afghanistan; two, preventing a future Taliban regime from being a pawn of Rawalpindi; three, making sure that the Pakistan-backed anti-India terrorist groups do not get support from the Taliban. In the past, India chose not to engage the Taliban (New Delhi had backed the Northern Alliance) and the costs were dear when the Taliban was in power. This time, New Delhi seems to be testing another policy."

The Taliban spokesman described the current government as "moribund" and referred to the country as the "Islamic emirate" - an indication that the group envisaged a theocratic basis for governing the country and were unlikely to agree to Afghan government demands for election.

Self doubts, shame and remorse are coursing through US after its troops left Bagram Air base at the dead of midnight last week, even without informing local Afghan Commanders. The picture of Afghan troops surrendering to Taliban without fight amid unfolding chaos, where large number of families have crossed over to neighbouring countries, ie Tajikistan, Uzbekistan and Iran. This is triggering questions from from security analysts including US lawmakers about imminent civil war and return of terrorism.

8

Demography of Afghanistan also adds Fuel to The Fire

While the Afghanistan National Defence and Security Forces, mostly funded by the United States and NATO, have put up resistance in some parts of the country, Afghan government troops overwhelmingly appear to have given up the ghost.

As reported there are approximately 350000 soldiers plus 40000 special force with Afghanistan, who supposed to have been trained by NATO forces as against Approximately 50000 Talibans, yet their performance is dismal. Afghans have over hundred aircrafts, but not used.

President Ashraf Ghani insists that Afghan security forces are fully capable of keeping insurgents at bay, but more than 1,000 Afghan troops fled over the border to Tajikistan in recent days, and there have also been reports of more soldiers seeking refuge in Pakistan and Uzbekistan to escape the fighting. This is mainly because of lack of mutual trust due to tribals rivalries, which adversely affects soldiers moral also.

While sectarianism is one cut of endangered "minority" status in Afghanistan, ethnicity is the other. Therefore, the Tajik and Uzbek, who may be essentially of Sunni denomination, are not spared the wrath of the Taliban or the Islamic State-Khorasan Province. Such persistent animus and diminishment led the Hazaras to form their own militias like the now-fragmented, Abdul Ali Mazari's Hezb-e-Wahdat, or the comparatively new Hazara warlord, Abdul Ghani Alipoor, who is now popularly seen as an effective vanguard against the fury of the Taliban. But these ethnic warlords are recklessly volatile, fickle and known to shift allegiances with the proverbial "exchange of suitcases", exposing their community to severe persecution. The endless cycle of sectarian wars in Afghanistan was exemplified by the reprisal attacks by the Taliban in Mazar-i-Sharif township in 1998 — thousands of Hazaras were searched out and killed in a systemic house-to-house killing frenzy as the Taliban was believed to shoot "anything that moved". As always, Pakistani hand in the Talibani advance was omnipresent as many Pakistani soldiers had accompanied the Taliban march. The Hazaras were apparently made to pay a price for the killing of several thousand Taliban soldiers a year earlier, after a failed attempt by the Taliban to takeover Mazar-i-Sharif in 1996.

Across the unaccepted borders with Pakistan, the Shias and Hazaras in particular, face the brunt of terror groups like Lashkar-e-Jhangvi, who remain committed to exterminate the Shias. These virulent sectarian groups have close ideological ties with the Taliban (on both sides) and have conducted spectacular and deadly attacks against the Shias — even the suicide bomber who killed former Pakistani Prime Minister Benazir Bhutto (who too was a Shia) belonged to Lashkar-e-Jhangvi. Quetta in Baluchistan is home to biggest settlement of the oppressed Hazaras in Pakistan, as also the unfortunate killing ground for most sectarian terror attacks — relaying the inevitable dangers of the State recklessly pandering to majoritarian-sectarianism to solidify itself. However, the dangers to suchlike "minorities" are multiplied when the sovereign Government itself runs the risk of passing on to the likes of the Taliban, which seems likely with the leaving of the US/NATO troops from Afghanistan.

The first port of societal destabilisation in a second Taliban regime in Afghanistan will be Pakistan, undoubtedly. Just recently the Pakistanis got a taste of pandering to the homegrown extremist sentiment with the embarrassing capitulation towards Tehreek-e-Labbaik Pakistan (TLP). Now, if the TLP which cannot even remotely be compared to the Taliban in terms of sheer firepower or ferocity could bring Islamabad to its knees, then having Afghanistan run by the Taliban who respect no international law or authority, will be a completely different ball game.

Meanwhile, the Taliban have seized other major border crossings, in Herat, Farah and Kunduz provinces in the north and west, threatening regional security. Taking to Twitter, Afghanistan vice president Amrullah Saleh said that the Taliban were forcing members of a small ethnic minority to either convert to Islam or leave their homes in the northern province of Badakhshan. The Taliban's rapid advances have also caused concern for the rights of women and girls as they were barred from school and most work under the group's harsh version of Islamic law.

The control of the border crossing between the Pakistani town of Chaman and the Afghan town of Wesh could be the most strategic objective they have captured so far amid rapid gains across the country. Taliban militants have taken down the Afghan government flag from atop the 'Friendship Gate' and hoisted Taliban flag. Taliban has reportedly captured Afghanpost, on Pakistan border where soldiers fled leaving Rs 300 crores to Talibans.

For the people of Afghanistan, it is a worrying time. The Taliban, who have been accused of various human rights and cultural abuses, support punishments such as public executions of convicted murderers - as well as banning television, music and becinema, and disapproving of girls over 10 going to school.

9

The Surge in Militias is a Recipe For Disaster

It is very painful and unpleasant to be abandoned, that is just what the United States of America has done to Afghanistan, and done so, for the second time." Integral to the act of abandonment is the selfishness of not caring about those 'abandoned'.

Taliban forces have achieved their most symbolic, if not the most important, victory in southern Kandahar province as they establish their control over Panjwai district. The region, which is the birthplace of the Taliban movement, has also been the venue of fierce battles against North Atlantic Treaty Organization forces for more than a decade. It fell to the Taliban hours after the Americans vacated the Kandahar military base.

Recent setbacks on the battlefield have exposed the vulnerability of the Afghan security forces without the support of foreign forces. Reports of soldiers surrendering to the Taliban without fighting in many places seem to have further dampened the morale of the Afghan security forces.

Vice President of Afghanistan Mr Saleh had posted on Twitter that Pakistan Airforce had issued an official warning to the Afghan army and AF that any move to dislodge the Taliban from Spin Boldak area in Kandhar province, will be faced and repelled by Pak Airforce. He also claimed to have the evidence of Pak Airforce supporting Talibans capture vital crossings.

Some other developments such as the emergence of regional militias under different warlords have also raised the spectre of civil war, with many predicting the fragmentation of Afghanistan along ethnic lines thus sucking neighbouring countries into the conflict. It is almost back to the Afghan situation in the 1990s.

The situation in Afghanistan has become more volatile with the Taliban launching a blistering compaign and capturing key districts of the country. As the Taliban stepped up attacks to gain control over Afghanistan, militant groups opposed to Pakistan and China have also increased their assualts. The Tehreek- e- Taliban which is against Pakistan is now active in tribal areas and Khyber Pakhtunkhwa province. Baluch seperatists are opposed to CPEC and China's interest in Gwadar port.

In Herat, Ismail Khan, once a dreaded warlord, has reportedly given a clarion call to his supporters to begin fighting the Taliban, with the man in his mid-70s offering to lead from the front, according to a Guardian report.

A key district in Herat province, home to tens of thousands of minority Shi'ite Hazaras was captured by fighters of the hardline Sunni Muslim insurgent group on Thursday as part of their strategy to oust Afghan forces and hold sway over critical border towns and trade routes.

Known as the Lion of Herat, Ismail Khan a veteran

Tajik commander is scheduled to hold a gathering to prepare his forces to fight against the Taliban and defend his power base in Herat, an official said, adding that several erstwhile anti-Taliban commanders were supporting the over-stretched Afghan forces to defend borders in the West and the North.

While the besieged Afghan President Ashraf Ghani is desperately clutching at straws, bargaining, and making fervent appeals for help, the former Afghan President Hamid Karzai slammed the "US legacy in Afghanistan of total disgrace and disaster".

Panjwai is located just across the border and the Taliban control there brings the war closer to Pakistan's frontiers. There have been reports of an exodus of Afghans as fighting intensifies. That could also lead to an influx of refugees into Pakistan.

In a meeting Monday with influential former anti-Soviet and anti-Taliban militia leaders, Ghani called on them to create a "united front" and support the Afghan security forces to "strengthen peace" and "safeguard the republic system." The Taliban rejects the current democratic governing system and seeks to install an Islamic one.

But the prospect of unleashing a hodgepodge of rogue warriors to repel their old enemies also raises the specter of civil war, a state of violent anarchy that Afghans remember all too well from the 1990s. The surge in militias is a recipe for disaster and a repetition of a dark history.

Chinese engaging discreetly with the rapidly advancing Taliban (promoted by the Pakistani 'establishment') and, more recently, of Turkey securing the rights to operate Kabul's Hamid Karzai International Airport and the unrelated talks of a $3 billion Chinese loan to the Turks have given credence to the possibility of a Triad in the making, and shaping future moves in places like Afghanistan. But this is not a seamless hypothesis as it is predicated on many simplistic assumptions of unrelated signals, post-takeover behaviour of the Taliban as also overlooking inherent fault lines within the Triad ideation.

A surge of Taliban wins in northern Afghanistan has caused some countries to close consulates in the region. The consulates of Germany, Turkey and Russia have been closed in Mazar- e- Shariff and Iran has restricted activities of its consulate.

In an emergency operation late Saturday, as many as 50 Indian diplomatic staff, including ITBP personnel, were evacuated from the Kandahar consulate, which is now operating only with the local staff, sources said""As of now India's missions in Kabul and Mazar-e-Sharif are operating with Indian diplomatic staff. Sources said India's.

India had already shut down its missions in Jalalabad and Herat in 2020, keeping in mind the deteriorating security condition in Afghanistan. However, it cited the pandemic as the official reason for the move.

In an interview to The Print, the Afghan envoy said the country's government is keen that India talk to those Taliban leaders who are willing to reconcile.

10

Taliban Surge in Afghanistan Gives Insomnia to Neighbors

There are some write ups doing round with personal assessments that Taliban are willing for power sharing, well I also tried to evaluate, but found such assessment too premature. Though this time Taliban shows a changed profile but not willing for power sharing as yet. There are still serious events in the pipeline to unfold. It is just the beginning of the play. It's my personal view.

Afghanistan is bordered by Pakistan to the East and South, Iran to the West, Turkmenistan, Uzbekistan and Tajikistan to the North and China to the North-East. Located at the heart of historic silk road, Afghanistan was long crossroads of commerce between Asian countries connecting them to Europe, and enhancing religious, cultural and commercial contacts. It is of strategic importance for Chinese to progress it's Belt and Road Initiative to Afghanistan, this will help China spread its influence across the world, from this base.

Afghanistan has cartographical contiguity with both Pakistan and China, as also co-religious denomination with

Turkey. Much has been speculated of Triad of Turkey, China and Pakistan assuming significance post Taliban takeover in Afghanistan, but it is not so seamless or linear, though each one has its own reasons to hold. To reach their own respective ends, China, Pakistan and Turkey have forged a hypothetical jointsmanship to counter the Taliban, but inherent fault lines remain.

History teaches that no one ever wins in Afghanistan, not even the native Afghans, who remain amongst the most deprived, denied, and regressive societies on the planet. As history is poised to repeat itself, for once, no one will be celebrating the exit of yet another empire, not even those who worked surreptitiously to support the forces inimical to the exiting empire.

The Taliban are not a monolithic, rationale or dependable entity that can be managed by any foreign power, leave alone a distinctively divergent set up like China. Afghanistan is perhaps the only country where all powers are wary of ensuing Taliban take over. The Taliban is not expected to show diplomatic dexterity or flexibility in dealing with any foreign power, especially a Communist power and a NATO power. The Taliban have stated plainly: "Turkey is a Muslim, brother country. However, since it's also a NATO member, if it remains in Afghanistan, it would not be any different from the US for us.

With the relentless surge of the Taliban towards Kabul, in a complete mockery of the socalled Doha Peace accord, there is growing palpitation in neighbouring Islamabad, Tehran, Dushanbe, Tashkent, Beijing and Delhi, and in Washington DC and Moscow, each for their own specific reasons.

Communist Party leaders in Beijing and the fundamentalist Taliban have little ideological common ground, but analysts say shared pragmatism could see mutual self-interest trump sensitive differences. For China, the risk does not come from who holds the power in Afghanistan, but from the risk of persistent instability.

China would rather have a moderate government like the current Ashraf Ghani set-up, as opposed to an unpredictable and puritanical Islamist dispensation of the Taliban. China abhors a power vacuum, especially on its borders, and maintaining stability after decades of war in its western neighbour will be Beijing's paramount consideration. China typically bides its time on the sidelines and then swoops in to exploit topical tensions and desperations towards exceptional concessions.

China can deal with the Taliban, but they still find the Taliban's religious agenda and motivations inherently discomforting. They have never been sure how willing or able the Taliban really are to enforce agreements on issues such as harbouring Uyghur militants.

Since the Aghan government has failed to provide security in places where Beijing wanted to make big investments, it now thinks it doesn't hurt if they invest in the Taliban and give them a chance. Back-door links with the Taliban through Pakistan have stretched back longer and "allowed China to avoid any major terrorist attack on its projects in Afghanistan.

Shiite Iran will remain a sectarian thorn for the Sunni-supremacist Taliban, as would the ethnically different nations of Uzbekistan and Tajikistan. Memories of the former 'empires' of the United States and Russia are too fresh to be forgiven, whereas history and perception within the Taliban ranks would rankle against India. The short 76-km border with China may be inactive and irrelevant for the Taliban ranks, but for the Chinese, the possible 'nurseries' of Melmastya could be a concern with Uighur separatist organisations like the East Turkestan Islamic Movement

(ETIM).

The unmatched, consistent, and vested role of Pakistan in supporting the Taliban, towards its own selfish doctrine of Strategic Depth in Afghanistan, is morally indefensible and incalculable in scale. As the chief protagonist of the movement, Pakistan was always unscrupulous, because it always had to play the patented Pakistani 'double game'.

China and Russia have tremendous influence on Central Asian countries such as Tajikistan, Uzbekistan and Turkmenistan, all three sharing borders with Afghanistan. A spillover of Taliban's extremist ideology into these Muslim-dominated countries would threaten to destabilise the entire region, which is not only Russia's sphere of influence but also a crucial part for China's Belt and Road Initiative (BRI).

About 650 US soldiers will remain in the country, mainly to protect embassy staff. They will also assist Turkish forces, who are on a non-combat mission to operate Kabul's Hamid Karzai International Airport. Ankara has hinted that it may deploy Syrian mercenaries in Afghanistan, a move that the Taliban has warned against.

11

Resurgence of Taliban Pushes India to Sidelines

Experts say the Taliban is stronger now than at any point since 2001. With up to eighty-five thousand full-time fighters, it controls one-fifth of the country and continues to launch attacks.

Taliban leadership is a moderate one (statement of Interior Minister Sheikh Rashid Ahmed) compared to the Taliban of 1996 when they publicly displayed the bodies of the slain Afghan president Najeeb Ulla and his brother.

The group is now believed to control roughly half of the nation's 400 districts, several important border crossings, and have laid siege to a string of vital provincial capitals. The Taliban have long appeared to be united, operating under an effective chain of command, and carrying out complex military campaigns despite perennial rumours of splits among the organisation's leadership. Questions remain over how firm of a hand the Taliban's leaders have with commanders on the ground and whether they will be able to convince them to abide by a potential agreement if signed.

Analysts disagree on the Taliban's motives and what the group seeks from intra-Afghan negotiations. Some experts and Afghans fear that the U.S.-Taliban agreement was just an attempt to remove foreign forces from Afghanistan and that it could spark a new conflict that would eventually allow the Taliban to regain control. For the Taliban, peace doesn't mean an end to the fighting, it means an end to the U.S. occupation.

"The Taliban's primary sources of revenue are opium poppy cultivation and narcotics, with a UN report estimating that it earned $400 million in 2018 from the illegal drug trade. It also levies taxes on commercial activities in its territories, such as farming and mining. It has supplemented its income with illicit mining, the extortion of local businesses, and donations from abroad, despite strict UN sanctions. Many experts say the Pakistani security establishment continues to provide Taliban militants sanctuary in the country's western tribal areas to try to counter India's influence in Afghanistan.

US strategy to train and equip Afghan army so that they could effectively deal with Talibans, has proved its potential when Taliban attacked Kandhar and were surprised by the weapons used by the Afghan army. The casualties of Jihadies were very high. It also bacame clear to Taliban that type of weapons they have are no match to the weapons provided by US to Afghan forces.

The Taliban present leadership reportedly is far less hardcore than what it was 25 years back. Though their ideology and motivation has not changed.

It is unlikely that the Pakistani military-jihadi complex will have the same level of control over the Taliban as that apparatus once did. Even if Rawalpindi somehow manages to exert control over Afghanistan's security policies, Pakistan will not get the same free pass from the West as it did under

America's Bill Clinton administration. Neither the United States nor the Gulf Arab states will turn a blind eye to cross-border terrorism. Pakistan will have to depend on China, Russia and Turkey for cover. Even if these countries decide to act as apologists for Pakistan-sponsored terrorism, they will do so in the face of opposition from the West. It's a wholly different world today.

The Talibanis too, beyond a point are inward looking and do not harbour internationalist agendas unlike other terror organisations like the Islamic State, Al Qaida etc. Though, Afghan forces are expecting the Taliban to attack key military installations such as Bagram at some point. The Afghan Armed Forces, comprising the National Army and the Air Force, have been equipped by the US with modern weapons and trained by multiple allies, including India.

Taliban is a current reality in Afghanistan. It is a party in the intra-Afghan talks which we believe should be a solution for normalisation and establishment of an inclusive government that should be involving all major ethnic groups.

India has been sidelined in Afghanistan due to its own policies that have failed to evolve in the face of rapidly changing regional circumstances, particularly America's and Russia's embrace of Pakistan. Since America, China, and Russia all talk to the Taliban nowadays.

India remains the only regional actor of relevance without official ties to the Taliban. New Delhi has politically principled reasons for this, but such a stance is arguably becoming counterproductive in the grand strategic sense when everyone else is already talking openly to the group.

What about India's influence over Afghanistan? Let's face it: It was not much to begin with. It is important to recognize this when considering what to do. The debate is caught in a false binary: Should India back the beleaguered Afghan national government or the rampant Taliban? Such a framing of the choice set neglects the important question of whether India's backing can tilt the scales enough for it to matter.

After the overthrow of the Taliban, India established diplomatic relations with the newly established democratic government, provided aid and participated in the reconstruction efforts. India has provided $650–750 million in humanitarian and economic aid, making it the largest regional provider of aid for Afghanistan.

Peace in Afghanistan is important for regional economic cooperation, connectivity and stability to prosper and endure. So far, India has played a significant role in promoting regional connectivity through ventures like the Chabahar Port Project, which connects Afghanistan with Central Asia and India.

India fears that at this stage in the war in Afghanistan between the Taliban and the government of President Ashraf Ghani if she openly takes sides with the latter then Indian interests in Afghanistan will become the target of Taliban violence and destruction. Hence, India's backdoor channel talks with the Taliban have been reportedly taking place.

India has suddenly become sidelined in Afghanistan. Regional processes are nowadays rapidly moving along a trajectory that doesn't appear to be in alignment with India's interests.

India's version of multi-alignment hasn't reaped expected dividends. This is probably because it's predicated on zero-sum geopolitical goals and not mutually beneficial geo-economic ones. India has also been unquestionably unsuccessful in isolating Pakistan since that neighbouring country now serves as the convergence point of American, Chinese, and Russian interests, which wasn't the case a year ago. These Great Powers all have a stake in Pakistan's stability for practical economic reasons, which will make it more challenging for India to pressure it in the future, potentially even through the Financial Action Task Force (FATF).

12

China's Despondency May Aggrevate Situation Faster in Afghanistan

With less than a month for the US military to move out of Afghanistan, a Taliban delegation was already in China on July 28 holding friendly 'talks' in Tianjin. Taliban seems to be China's new friend. Why? Because it makes for good business sense.

This is the first time a senior Taliban leader has visited China since the group launched an offensive to capture territories across Afghanistan, coinciding with the rapid drawdown of US and Nato forces

It seems that the People's Republic of China is in a hurry to grant legitimacy to Taliban. It was evident in the way that the PRC interacted with the Taliban group; akin to how it would welcome, and hold talks with genuine diplomatic missions from sovereign countries. Economy is what the People's Republic of China is betting on to bring Afghanistan into its web of influence; To make that happen Beijing seems ready to partner with anyone who can deliver the goods even if it be a regressive religio-political militia like the Taliban.

Interest of Beijing is China's ambitious Belt and Road initiative (BRI), which till now had not made much headway as far as Afghanistan was concerned. The BRI is a network of land and sea routes that, across 6 corridors, will span the Eurasian landmass and China has already invested more than $60 billion in one of the corridors - the China Pakistan Economic Corridor (CPEC) at the southern end of which sits the massive Gwadar port that China built in Balochistan, Pakistan. It is as part of the CPEC that China had for long been negotiating the construction of a Peshawar- Kabul highway that would link up Afghanistan with the BRI.

"Pakistan remained silent about a major terror attack, killing of nine Chinese workers and four others. A full-fledged Pakistani Army Division (34th Light Infantry Division), also known as Special Security Division (SSD), dedicated to protecting Chinese workers and assets of China Pakistan Economic Corridor (CPEC), has been operational since 2016. But this elaborate security cover has not deterred Pakistani groups opposing the perceived usurpation of their local rights, from repeatedly targeting the Chinese.

The Pakistani Taliban had claimed responsibility for targeting "locals and foreigners", though Baloch and Sindhi groups too have routinely targeted the Chinese. The embarrassment for the Pakistani Military in their inability to guarantee security to their "all-weather friends". The East Turkistan Islamic Movement (ETIM) terrorists who flee from Afghanistan to Pakistan may also conduct the terror attacks targeting Chinese.

The atheist Communist Party of China and the fundamentalist Taliban have little in common ideologically but shared mutual interests could form the basis of pragmatic if wary ties. The Chinese foreign minister met Taliban's political chief to discuss peace and reconciliation process and the way forward in Afghanistan. Baradar, who heads the Taliban's political office in Qatar and is the lead negotiator for talks with the US, is leading a nine-member Taliban delegation on a two-day visit to China.

While the Taliban may have tactically reassured the Chinese about the future, for now — but given their nativist, puritanical and irascible moorings, for them to spurn the beleaguered Uighurs in favour of Communist China will be impossible. The Chinese, too, are in a thick soup in the Af-Pak quagmire.

China on Wednesday told a Taliban delegation that it hopes the insurgent group will play a critical role in the reconstruction process of Afghanistan in the backdrop of US forces leaving the country. Statecouncillor and foreign minister Wang Yi urged the Taliban to crack down on the East Turkestan Islamic Movement (ETIM), an Islamic group it alleges is fuelling unrest and separatism in China's Xinjiang province from Afghanistan.

Over the centuries foreign powers have failed to control or stabilise Afghanistan. In the last half a century itself two Superpowers, first the USSR and now the US, have had to withdraw if not always in defeat but certainly not in a shower of glory. The overall trend is clearly unfavorable to the Afghan government, which could face an existential crisis if it isn't addressed and reversed.

Help has also come in the form of/ U.S. airstrikes in support of Afghan forces, despite/ the U.S./ no longer having aircraft based in Afghanistan. Officials have/ promised/ the strikes/ will continue unless the Taliban/ scale back their military offensive. "The Afghan air force, in particular, has/ been dependent on U.S. government contractors for maintenance and logistics./ But/ as of last month, it is reported that the number of contractors had been cut in half/ because of the ongoing U.S. withdrawal.

India faces the consequences of losing its investment of about three billion dollars in Afghanistan besides, AQIS, ISIS and Pakistani terrorists training their guns towards Kashmir. Apart from the above difficulties, if the current Afghan government loses power, then a large number of Afghan population may migrate to India. It should be noted that as per UNHCR, there were about 40,000 Afghan refugees in India till 2019.

In order to understand the implications for J&K, it is pertinent to understand the motivations and aspirations that beset Taliban per se, the track record of Taliban regime towards Kashmir, and the expected headwinds that will further warrant recalibration, in Taliban thinking, now. For starters beyond religiousity, the Taliban is bound by ethnicity of Pashtun clans that affords it a certain restricted, nativist and exclusivist agenda that is not global in outlook (unlike an Islamic State or Al Qaida). While its Pashtunwali code necessitates deeply revered principle like Melmastya (Hospitality) and Nenawate (Asylum), which were often used to justify sheltering other militant organisations – its own outreach, joining-of-ranks or jointsmanship in other religio-inspired battles across the battlefields of Middle East or even Kashmir, had been extremely limited.

13

US Troops Withdrawal from Iraq- Another scenario in the Offing

(Rivalries Between ISIS & Taliban Likely to Resurface in Afghanistan)

The Islamic State – also known as ISIS, ISIL, or Daesh – emerged from the remnants of al Qaeda in Iraq (AQI), a local offshoot of al Qaeda founded by Abu Musab al Zarqawi in 2004. It faded into obscurity for several years after the surge of U.S. troops to Iraq in 2007. But it began to reemerge in 2011. Over the next few years, it took advantage of growing instability in Iraq and Syria to carry out attacks and bolster its ranks.

The ideology of both the organisations are same, belong to same religious sect, but aims differ in that IS aspire for global influence whereas Taliban being locals only look for gaining control of Afghanistan. The laws of IS are more stringent and cruel than Taliban.

In 2015, ISIS expanded into a network of affiliates in at least eight other countries. Its branches, supporters, and affiliates increasingly carried out attacks beyond the borders of its so-called caliphate. The Baghdadi era of ISIS ended on October 26, 2019, when the leader was killed in a U.S. raid in northern Syria.

Islamic State (IS) rarely makes the mainstream media headlines these days. After losing the last of their territory during the Battle of Baghuz Fawqani in early 2019, the "caliphate was declared "defeated". However, 2020 saw a significant growth in IS attacks in their traditional heartlands of Syria and Iraq, as well as a growing presence in the Afghanistan-Pakistan region and across large parts of the African continent. Despite the loss of territory, the ideology of ISIS was not defeated, and although it's difficult to put a precise number on their manpower, there is evidence that they are re-establishing themselves in the Middle East.

Because the Islamic State first established itself in Afghanistan by recruiting among Taliban dissidents and Afghan Salafist networks, the Taliban remain wary of new ISIS offshoots emerging from these disaffected militants. In northern Afghanistan in particular, Taliban authorities have repeatedly purged commanders they suspect of harboring sympathies for the Islamic State. They have also arrested or expelled clerics whom they suspect of recruiting for their ISIS rivals, whose forces may have splintered, but are still seen as a significant threat to the Taliban's mission.

In these ways, it is clear that the Islamic State is a real threat to both the Taliban and to the success of the peace process. But in other ways, the rivalry with the Islamic State has actually given the Taliban an excuse for their hard-line stances in Doha, strengthening their negotiating position and even affording the movement a degree of international credibility.

The campaign to suppress the Islamic State is necessary to protect the broader peace process. Despite its reduced capabilities, the Islamic State retains the potential to act as a spoiler and poses a significant residual terrorist threat, with the capability and motivation to attack key figures or events that could cause maximum disruption to the negotiations. Such an imminent threat requires strong security countermeasures and measures to restore confidence in the peace process among the public. For instance, Afghan government authorities could follow up on attacks like the one on Kabul University by conducting forensic examinations and maximizing transparency in its reporting on which extremist group is responsible for the attack. Confidence in the peace process may depend upon clearly distinguishing whether the Islamic State or the Taliban are responsible for specific attacks, thus exposing or ruling out false flags.

From the outset, Mansoor considered the Islamic State a threat to Taliban unity because it proposed an alternative vision for an Islamist state in the region, thereby challenging the Taliban's jihadist monopoly in Afghanistan. He responded to this nascent rival by encouraging the Islamic State's Afghanistan-based recruits to travel to Syria and Iraq instead—and giving them the money to do so. He lobbied the Islamic State's leader, Abu Bakr al-Baghdadi, to reject oaths of allegiance from those who had volunteered for the local franchise, and even took decisive military action against emerging Islamic State pockets in Afghanistan.

Islamic State would take the opportunity to recruit Taliban fighters, who are highly motivated and committed to sustaining the jihad, and may feel alienated by the Taliban leaders' apparent moderate posture in the peace process. In particular, if the Taliban were to agree to an early cease-fire, the Islamic State would be bound to take that chance to present itself as the true heir of the Afghan jihad, split the Taliban's membership and recruit defectors from their ranks.

The Islamic State still poses a lingering threat to peace and stability in Afghanistan, so it remains a key consideration for the Taliban, even shaping their priorities and tactics during their ongoing negotiations with the Afghan government and the United States. Ultimately, the rivalry between these groups reflects the Taliban's enduring motivations: dominating the jihad in Afghanistan and, with it, the country itself.

ISIS attacks in Iraq and Syria have increased significantly in 2020, demonstrating both a capacity and a willingness on ISIS's part to retake territory, populations, and resources.

In the wake of COVID-19 and the drawdown of U.S. forces, security gaps have worsened, allowing ISIS to move more freely, conduct prison breaks, carry out more sophisticated attacks, and smuggle fighters across borders.

President Joe Biden says US forces will end their combat mission in Iraq by the end of this year, but will continue to train and advise the Iraqi military. There are currently 2,500 US troops in Iraq helping local forces counter what remains of the Islamic State group.

Political parties aligned to Iran have demanded the withdrawal of all forces from the US-led global coalition against IS, despite the continuing threat posed by the Sunni jihadist group. The US presence in Iraq has become a major issue since top Iranian General Qasem Soleimani and the leader of an Iran-backed Shia Muslim militia were killed in a US drone strike in the capital Baghdad last year.

Shia militias have meanwhile been accused by the US of carrying out hundreds of rocket, mortar and drone attacks on Iraqi military bases that host coalition forces in an apparent attempt to pressure them to leave.

14

Fall of Kabul Looks Imminent-US Too To Blame : (Weak Defence of Afghan Cities Affords Walk Over To Taliban)

It has become rather unpalatable for any military thinker that despite there being vast disparity between Afghan forces and Taliban in terms of strength, weapons, training, and air support etc, how Taliban is overrunning large parts of Afghan Cities with speed and impunity. US totally failed to train Afghan forces to be battle worthy in long 20 years, they rather made them dependent on US support and once they left, the system nearly collapsed.

I attempted to fathom, the concept of Afghan city defence system, which is collapsing without putting any resistance, and found it utterly weak, which I am sharing with the readers in the text. The views are totally my personal.

There were mistakes made and are still being made by the United States in the way it didn't nail down its planning and its post-withdrawal parameters. But there has also been a state of either denial or negligence on the Afghan government's part in not throwing itself into a comprehensive plan to steel itself for what was coming.

All of a sudden in one week, nine out of 34 provincial capitals fall to the Taliban, or seem like they're on the verge of falling the answer is, well, half of the country slipped out of the government's control in the last three months, and it no longer had a buffer protecting those provincial capitals, which were these village outposts and district centers standing in the way.

The Taliban is rapidly overrunning large parts of Afghanistan. Over the past few days, Taliban fighters have reportedly taken over nine provincial capitals. The siege comes after a relentless, monthslong offensive in the country that has stretched Afghan government forces. Since the US began withdrawing its troops from the country at the start of May, the Taliban has swept through about half of Afghanistan's 400 districts.

Starting about three months ago, in late May and then June, picking up speed in July, the Taliban launched an offensive campaign that has swept across the country in a way that has been unprecedented. There are a little over 400 districts across Afghanistan; almost all of them have what's called a district administrative center.

The Afghan government has pointed to this district center map as a means of demonstrating their authority, when in reality, their only presence or assertion of authority might be a district center where they have a couple buildings that are protected by a small military or police force, or sometimes just a militia that's outfitted and paid by the government. And that's it. That is the only government that exists in that entire district, for miles around in any direction.

In some places, these remote villages and outposts that the Afghan government had been trying to prop up had become surrounded. The Afghan government couldn't get them ammunition. It couldn't get them food a lot of the time. A lot of the people at these outposts, they weren't getting regularly paid. Their families weren't getting their paychecks consistently from month to month. And so you're talking about a terrible level of morale among the Afghan government's security forces.

In districts where maybe 10 or 20 Taliban fighters would show up, they would have already laid the groundwork with a disinformation campaign.Taliban would tell local residents, "There are 2,000 more Taliban fighters, and they're right behind us. They are on the way, and we're going to burn down your village, we're going to kill everybody; it's hopeless, you're surrounded, so you may as well just run away.

The fact is, the government has either been kicked out of or abandoned more than 200 of the 400 districts in the country. That's happened in just the last three months. Something that's important here as important as the Taliban capturing provincial capitals is that the Taliban has begun to capture large, commercial cross-border customs points.

It's still too fluid to say they're consolidating anything. What we can say is that they're amassing huge numbers of their fighters to try and encircle or surround some of these cities. They're doing it in multiple regions of the country: in the north, in the southwest. In some places, the government is pushing them back more effectively than others.

The Taliban's approach has been to demonstrate Kabul's weaknesses and to try to pressure it to collapse. The question is going to be whether or not they continue to squeeze from the outside in, or whether they move to squeeze Kabul directly. It's not obvious yet which they're going to opt for.

At some point in the last three months, the Afghan government seemed to realize that was, in fact, what it needed to do. But it made that realization far too late. If the decision had been made earlier, it could have been explained to the Afghan public in a way that might have mitigated the panic that you see spreading across the country now. It also could have prevented a lot of operational-level losses. Untold amounts of ammunition and military equipment have been left behind in these 200 districts where military forces have picked up and left.

Militarily, the Afghan government has the advantage. It has an air force that is still functioning, for now. It has incredibly capable special forces, even though they're stretched quite thin and are often the ones sent to do the fighting around the country. In spite of all its challenges, they do have the technical military capacity. The question is about political leadership and a sense of unity.

Much of Afghan society is still decentralized, and you've got a government attempting to centralize, but in a way that isolates or alienates many local communities. The cost of centralization has been the government's inability to actually establish buy-in and cooperation and support from whole regions of the country.

15

Islamic Emirate of Afghanistan - 'Not Yet Recognised': Talibans Policies will Determine It's Stability

Kabul fell to the Taliban in a swift and seemingly bloodless take over on Aug 15, and it's President Ashraf Ghani flew to Tajikistan. The shameful conduct of Afghan security forces, made job easy for Taliban to overrun a country just in matter of a few days. The US global reputation and geopolitical equities also went in flames following the fall of Kabul to Taliban. Anger and shame coursed through in the political circle. The world biggest military power spent 20 years training an army that collapsed in 20 days.

The speed of the Taliban's advance and the lack of resistance faced so far have come as a surprise to all sides including the Taliban leaders themselves. But this should not blind anyone to the fact that throughout modern history, no single political, religious or ethnic group, regardless of its size, has been able to enjoy full hegemony and legitimacy across a piece of land without reaching a political settlement with all other groups.

Chaotic collapse of Afghanistan's existing institutions, including the army, police and civil service will leave the Taliban presiding over a nightmare scenario akin to Iraq and Syria. The group will find that many intellectuals, investors, and people with technical capacities have long left the country to Turkey, the UAE, Pakistan, and India.

The Taliban's rapid advance has ousted some of Afghanistan's traditional warlords: Abdul Rashid Dostum has fled to Uzbekistan, Atta Mohammad Noor is reported to have left the country, and Ismail Khan is under house arrest in Herat. With them out of the political scene, the many fragmented factions in Kabul are now no longer talking in the same disparate tones. They are doing their best to cast aside their differences and present a united front.

However, the irony of the Taliban spreading its control so widely and so quickly is that its ability to control, secure and, most importantly, supply those areas will be tested for the first time. The overnight transformation in the movement's responsibilities is huge – from a guerrilla force reliant on what supplies can be offered to it by local communities it is turning into an authority in control of complex urban spaces.

The Taliban must protect all state institutions, including the civil service, and do its very best to ensure they continue to function. This is a major lesson from Iraq and Syria: Any transitional arrangement should not undo the armed forces or civil service. Taliban leaders, who have issued declarations of amnesty and ordered fighters to protect community assets and refrain from acts of vengeance in the recently captured districts.

Taliban must improve its relationship with the international community of donors. It could begin to do so by protecting their missions inside the country and making sure it follows a zero-tolerance policy against all forms of human rights abuses, in particular those directed against women and girls.

For India, Taliban take over of Afghanistan makes environment challenging, apart from jeopardizing it's investment in Afghanistan including the flagship Slama Dam, the chances of terrorist groups shifting to bases accross the Durand line, with the inbuilt fear of its spillover into Kashmir.

The relationship is born of necessity rather than preference. Many Chinese officials and analysts have doubts about how modernized the Afghan Taliban will ever be. Although some in China assess that the Taliban have become more pragmatic, there is no guarantee for what their policy will look like, especially regarding relations with radical Islamic organizations in the region.

It is unlikely that the Pakistani military-jihadi complex will have the same level of control over the Taliban as the apparatus once did. Even if Rawalpindi somehow manages to exert control over Afghanistan security policies, Pakistan will not not get the same free pass from the West as it did under America's Bill Clinton administration. Pakistan will have to depend on China, Russia and Turkey for cover.

Taliban stated its willingness to undertake a peaceful transfer of power in Afghanistan. This is being met with a sigh of relief by the international community. But guards should not drop. This is not noblesse oblige. It is a tactic that buys the Taliban time to consolidate its gains from a rapid sweep of provincial capitals. It is a tactic to avoid international condemnation, sidestep an emergency resolution at the UN Security Council, and ensure aid distribution continues so the group is not blamed for a humanitarian crisis.

The Taliban victory in Afghanistan is now all but complete. The speed of the collapse of the central government and its military has been stunning and will spur endless postmortems about what went wrong and who is to blame. But the immediate situation demands attention to minimize a massive humanitarian disaster.

The international community must state unequivocally to the Taliban that atrocities against women and girls will be met with harsh sanctions. Regional actors that have aided and abetted the Taliban over the past two decades should face similar consequences.

Taliban are not monolithic, rationale or dependable entity that can be managed by any foreign power, leave alone a distinctively divergent set up like China or Pak. Afghanistan is perhaps the only country where all powers are wary of ensuing Taliban take over. The Taliban is not expected to show diplomatic dexterity or flexibility in dealing with any foreign power.

16

Taliban Returns To Afghanistan
(India's Strategic Options)

Taliban has managed a walk over in Afghanistan as latter's army shamefully gave up resistance for the fear of reprisal. Unfortunately some leading regional powers are obscenely courting the blight of Taliban, which is reimposing a repressive, regressive, Islamist dogma on Afghanistan. It hasn't taken very long for the unbridled bigotry of Taliban to embolden other Islamists extremists in Afghanistan and beyond.

Indian interests in Afghanistan has been its importance for regional connectivity. The whole idea of the US New Silk Road Strategy was to link Central Asia and South Asia (especially India) via Afghanistan through trade, transit and energy routes. From the Indian side, investments at the Chabahar port in Iran and the Zaranj-Delaram Road in Afghanistan were part of this strategy.

The new security and economic architecture in Afghanistan is going to be different form the one followed by Kabul in the last 20 years. The new influencers, viz. China, Pakistan, Russia and Iran, will be happy to see that the US influence reduces further. China and Pakistan will also try to minimise Indian engagement. Afghanistan will continue to be important for regional connectivity. But now the focus may change towards China's Belt and Road Initiative (BRI) and the Gwadar port in Pakistan.

India has not been in a position to influence the outcome in Afghanistan, it is time for New Delhi to carefully monitor the evolving situation and wait for the opportunity for new engagements. The Taliban government, even under Pakistani influence, will need broader recognition and economic opportunities arising from Indian linkages.

The Indian-built projects, including the already built Zaranj-Delaram Highway and Salma Dam, are already under Taliban control, and a cloud hangs over those under construction, including check-dams, schools and urban projects.

India remains the only regional actor of relevance without official ties to the Taliban. New Delhi has politically principled reason for this, but such a stance is arguably becoming counter productive in the grand Strategic sense when everyone else is already talking openly to the group. Iran, Russia, China and Pakistan—embraced the Taliban, with the common goal of evicting the United States from the region, and securing their interests.

In the coming years, India will find itself in a relatively disadvantageous position in Afghanistan. This is the prize India has to pay for going too close to the United States and certain errors in its own policy judgements.

Talibans swift ascend may rewrite geopolitical alliances, where Pak would have bigger arena to play against India and there could be rise in terrorism. Though this would amount to playing again with fire which burns those who try to kindle it. Also a new alliance with Taliban led Afghanistan at the core, including China, Pak, Russia, Turkey, Qatar and possibly Iran, is another point of serious concern for india.As of now India should also wait and watch before deciding on an option, till then it should beef up its defence to handle a possible wave of Jihadhism and have retaliatory action against Pak who would be conduit for these Jihadhies.

Pakistan has long played a paradoxical role in Afghanistan: a nominal US ally in its "war on terror" that has for decades been accused of covertly providing the Taliban with the support to withstand the Nato-backed military campaign particularly via its powerful Inter-Services Intelligence agency. Pakistan has plenty to lose from the Taliban's ascendancy, which risks triggering problems ranging from a flood of refugees to a resurgence of domestic terrorism linked to the insurgents, which has killed thousands of Pakistanis.

Jihadi groups operating in and around Pakistan, most notably the Pakistani Taliban or TTP, "consider the Taliban's takeover of Afghanistan as a larger ideological victory. That portends instability in the region in the longer run.Somesympathised with the Islamists' extreme ideology, while others deemed it an indispensable asset to counter India. Some in India see this as a loss for Delhi and a big win for Pakistan.

It was too simplistic a view, because the Pashtun-led Taliban has never recognised the border between Afghanistan and Pakistan, creating discomfort for Islamabad. But it's also true that the Taliban's rule in Afghanistan gives Pakistan strategic depth against India.

India was never as big a player in Afghanistan as Pakistan, the US or Russia. But Delhi has always been involved in promoting security and cultural ties. Thousands of Afghans are in India for education, work or medical treatment.

So there are no easy options for India, but its decisions will have consequences on regional peace and global geopolitics.India's best option at the moment seems to be keep a channel of communication open with the Taliban. But it will be an uneasy relationship, considering the history between the Taliban and Delhi.

The biggest challenge India will face is whether to recognise the Taliban government or not. The decision will get tough, especially if Moscow and Beijing decide to acknowledge the Taliban government in some form. Russia and Iran also seem to be on the same trajectory - neither has evacuated its embassy, and both nations' diplomats are still working in Kabul.

China also has economic interests in Afghanistan, which can help fulfil its ever-growing need for minerals, but more importantly it can pressure the Taliban to ban the East Turkestan Islamic Movement (ETIM), which it blames for unrest in its Muslim-dominated Xinjian province, to operate on Afghan soil.

Even though the Taliban's takeover of Afghanistan was rapid, it is not likely the militants will get their hands on the central bank's $10 billion in assets, including the $1.3 billion in gold reserves. The reason is that most of the $10 billion worth of assets are stored outside of Afghanistan, according to one Afghan official. However, the Taliban most likely did get its hands on the DAB's foreign currency cash holdings worth around $362 million, which were being stored at the bank's head offices, branches, and the presidential palace.

Since the money for Afghanistan drying up with the

US exit, Pakistan is not in a position to financially prop up the new Afghan regime. This opens up possibility of other countries like India making deals with the new dispensation in Kabul. Plus given Afghanistan's diverse ethnic matrix, a non-Pashtun insurgency may materialise with the use of left over weapons by Afghanarmy ,should Taliban seek to return to its old ways and suppress minorities. Taken together, Pakistan's influence over shaping the future of Afghanistan should not be over estimated. Regional countries like India have many cards to play here.

Afghanistan economy is heavily reliant on aid and loans, which provides leverage against Taliban. Afghanistan economy is acutely vulnerable to a shift in the stance of Western donors and Japan. It's nominal GDP is close to, $20 billions, which is in the ballpark of the J&K economy. Afghanistan is highly sensitive to multiple risks. A mere 12 pc of the land is arable which supports 70 pc of the population. However there is one area that holds a rich promise, ie untapped minerals wealth of over $1 trillion. It includes gold, copper and perhaps most importantly lithium, that holds the key for the world electric vehicle future, which attracts China the most.

17

How Long Can Panjshir Resist Taliban Onslaught ?

The Panjshir Valley has repeatedly played a decisive role in Afghanistan's military history, as its geographical position almost completely closes it off from the rest of the country. The only access point to the region is through a narrow passage created by the Panjshir River, which can be easily defended militarily. Most of the valley's up to 150,000 inhabitants belong to the Tajik ethnic group, while the majority of the Taliban are Pashtuns.The region, located 150 kilometers (93 miles) northeast of the capital, Kabul, now hosts some senior members of the ousted government, like the deposed Vice President Amrullah Saleh.

Famed for its natural defenses, the region tucked into the Hindu Kush mountains never fell to the Taliban during the civil war of the 1990s, nor was it conquered by the Soviets a decade earlier. The valley is also known for its emeralds, which were used in the past to finance the resistance movements against those in power.

After the withdrawal of the Soviet Union in 1989, civil war broke out in Afghanistan, which the Taliban ultimately won. However, Massoud and his United Front (also known as the Northern Alliance) succeeded in controlling not only the Panjshir Valley but almost all of northeastern Afghanistan up to the border with China and Tajikistan, thus protecting the region from the Taliban.

The Panjshir Valley is Afghanistan's last remaining holdout where anti-Taliban forces seem to be working on forming a guerrilla movement to take on the Islamic fundamentalist group. Since mid-August, forces opposed to the rule of the Afghan Taliban have gathered in the valley under the leadership of Ahmad Massoud, son of the famed Afghan resistance fighter Ahmad Shah Massoud. Panjshir resistance was announced and the flag of the Northern Alliance was hoisted in the valley.

Ahmad Massoud's father, Ahmad Shah Massoud, nicknamed the "lion of the Panjshir," blocked Soviet forces in the 1980s and the Taliban in the 1990s from conquering the narrow and almost impenetrable valley It has in effect one main road in and out. His 32-year-old son, who was trained at Britain's military academy Sandhurst and was taught war studies at King's College, London, hopes to emulate his father.

Massoud has been storing arms and material for the past two years, since the U.S. opened talks with the Taliban. His local militia has been boosted, his aides say, with an influx of a few thousand former Afghan army soldiers, including members of special forces units, and volunteers from other militias from northern and western Afghanistan. There are about 10,000 strong force gathered to defend.

Without outside support, military experts say it is hard to estimate how long Massoud can keep the Taliban out of the valley, and resupply will be difficult. The Panjshir has no airport and the Taliban in theory now surround the valley "Nobody can answer the question 'how long?"

Amid reports of the anti-Taliban force gaining strength,

training security forces in Panjshir province, the last Taliban-free area of Afghanistan, analysts have said that if the Taliban launch a full-scale attack, the anti-Taliban fighters will have to struggle. Though the takeover might not be without resistance as it happened in the rest of the country, the fighters gathered there will have to struggle if the Islamist hardliners launch a full-scale attack. The resistance for the moment is just verbal because the Taliban have not yet tried to enter the Panjshir.

A key risk for the Taliban with the resistance in the Panjshir is the unraveling of local surrender pacts the Islamists struck with tribal elders and local warlords.

The Taliban are dispatching hundreds of fighters to the Panjshir Valley, 150 kilometers north of the Afghan capital, Kabul, to try to stamp out an emerging resistance.The resistance for the moment is just verbal because the Taliban have not yet tried to enter the Panjshir. The Taliban only need to lock down the Panjshir, they don't even have to go in there.

Talibs have massed forces near the entrance of Panjshir a day after they got trapped in ambush zones of neighboring Andarab valley. If Taliban surround Panjshir from all sides and I don't think Massoud's son can resist much more than a couple of months. For the moment, he does not have any really strong support.

The Panjshir Valley is Afghanistan's last remaining holdout where anti-Taliban forces seem to be working on forming a guerrilla movement to take on the Islamic fundamentalist group.

Massoud told Reuters that he did not want war. We want to make the Taliban realize that the only way forward is through negotiation," he said by telephone. He said his fighters are ready to fight. They want to resist any totalitarian regime.

18

Afghanistan Likely To Be The Epicenter of Terrorism

(Insight into Existing Terror Threats)

The latest suicide bombings at Kabul airport have horribly complicated the situation in Afghanistan. There is no denying the fact that US royally messed up the issue by pulling out troops before completing civilian evacuation which was a huge mistake, and prematurely leaving the Bagram airbase which Taliban soon occupied and released 5000 prisoners including many dreaded ISIS and other terrorists who were housed there.

The recent ghastly and audacious strikes at Kabul airport highlight the menace of ISIS-k and other boundary defying terrorist groups to the stability of not just Afghanistan but it's extended neighborhood. Being secretive and relatively small in numbers, these outfits can not topple a regime, like Taliban did in Afghanistan, but they can create nuisance by killing innocent people and disturb the existing peace and order. India would soon need to have contingency in place if Afghanistan becomes a terror heaven, it will involve strengthening of security and restoring normalcy in Kashmir.

It seems inevitable that the Taliban will allow al Qaeda, ISIS, and other terrorist groups we haven't even heard of yet to find sanctuary in Afghanistan. Taliban cemented its control over Afghanistan this weekend, raising concerns that a weakened al Qaeda and other terrorist groups could stage a comeback in the wake of the chaotic U.S. military withdrawal.

The Taliban's fighting forces in northern Afghanistan include Uzbek and Tajik nationals, who have been involved in Islamist insurgencies in Central Asia. The Taliban has ties to jihadists from Xinjiang, in China. It also includes within its rank large numbers of jihadists with viciously anti-Shi'a beliefs. To make things worse, the Taliban has close links with narcotics traffickers and other criminal cartels.

Al- Qaeda remains closely allied with and embedded with in the Taliban. The Taliban provide an umbrella group and operating space for about 20 terrorist groups broadly aligned with Al-Qaida and Taliban objectives. Many of these militants in Afghanistan were displaced by security operations in the tribal areas of Pakistan. The total number of foreign terrorist fighters in Afghanistan is estimated at 10000 to 15000. The Taliban is inseparable from al-Qaeda, with cultural, familial and political obligations from which it will remain unable to fully abandon, even were its leadership sincere in seeking to do so.

There have been reports already of Islamic State elements present in Afghanistan and if they get the opportunity to put down infrastructure and train then that will pose a threat to the west more widely. Islamic State and the Taliban have fought over territory because of political differences and said a Taliban military victory could have a negative impact on Islamic State's presence in the country. ISIS in Afghanistan is largely underground and clandestine.

Islamic State in Iraq and the Levant-Khorasan has expanded its presence in several provinces of Afghanistan and strengthened its positions in and around Kabul. Its leaders also hope to attract intransigent Taliban and other militants who reject the agreement between the United States and the Taliban and to recruit fighters from Iraq, the Syrian Arab Republic and other conflict zones. Ultimately what both al-Qaeda and the Islamic State group need to thrive is a chaotic, unstable situation. All the signs indicate that in Afghanistan, they are about to get it.

There is unanimity among security experts that the recent developments in Afghanistan will have implications in the insurgency in Kashmir even as they expressed varying degrees of threat to the situation in the Valley.

With the Taliban in power in much of Afghanistan, India has other concern as well. One worry is that group such as Lashkar- e- Taiba and Jaise-e-Mohammad that have been keeping bases and training ground along the Southern provinces that borders Pakistan could have more ungoverned spaces to carry out attacks against India. The Taliban control will also mean a bigger hand for Pakistan military and intelligence agencies to influence outcome for the country, which will mandate a much smaller role for Indian development and infrastructure work that has won it goodwill over the past 20 years.

Pakistan may shift terror training camps of Jaish and Lashkar from PoK to Afghanistan for avoiding international scrutiny and for claiming that it has no role in the violence in Kashmir. It suits Pakistan. Anti-India terror groups would get safe havens in Afghanistan.

Pakistan's intelligence agency ISI may also try to

persuade the Taliban to help them on the issue of Kashmir. But, the pressure on the Taliban to obey the ISI will be less as it has already made a strong comeback in Afghanistan. According to information, Pakistan's terrorist organizations Lashkar-e-Taiba and Lashkar-e-Jahangvi already have links with Taliban, and these terrorist organizations have collaborated with Taliban in many villages of Afghanistan and some areas of Kabul to create check posts.

In short term, the fallout probably won't be huge even though India s borders on the map, extend to Afghanistan, POK in fact lies between the two countries, which provides something of a geographical cushion. In recent years, Pakistan has scaled back cross border infiltration by terrorist groups, not because of Afghanistan but because of fears of war, which it's economy is I'll poised to face. As long as Pakistan keeps Jihadhi tap shut, things in Kashmir will remain stable.

There are security concerns that Afghanistan might become the first epicenter of Islamic terrorism which has a state, they have access to all the weapons which Americans have supplied and also the weapons of 3 lakh plus Afghan National Army personnel.

Even then, their hostility towards India was found to be driven more by the agenda of the Pakistani military-jihadi complex and less by any intrinsic animosity towards us. In recent times, their adversarial position towards New Delhi has been in response to India's support for the Afghan government and, until recently, the refusal to talk to them.The fact that about 25 pc of terrorists operating in J&K in 1990s were from Afghanistan. Therefore not withstanding the goodwill shown by Taliban, India has to remain wary of Taliban.

For the Taliban, Uyghurs of China's northwest Xinjiang province are co- religionists just across the border. For many

Pashtuns of Pakistan's frontier region, the Pakistani army is an enemy that is oppressing their ethnic brethren across a colonial border they have never recognized. The Russians, for their part, would not mind their Chinese allies getting a bloody nose. The Chinese, being nobody's fools, are unlikely to want to be the latest foreign power to enjoy the delights of Afghan politics. Each of these fault lines presents New Delhi with levers.

The Islamic State Khorasan formed in late 2014 and operates as an ISIS affiliate in Afghanistan and Pakistan. Khorasan is a historical term for a region that includes present-day Afghanistan and parts of the Middle East and Central Asia. The group is also known as ISIS-K or IS-K. The ISIS offshoot is a more extreme rival of the Taliban. Experts say the Taliban is likely to try to root out the group. But some warned earlier this month that ISIS-K could benefit from a security vacuum as the Taliban tries to consolidate power.

IS-K is a far smaller group than the Taliban. The group had between 1,500 and 2,200 members in eastern Afghanistan in June, according to a report from a United Nations monitoring team, compared to roughly 75,000 Taliban fighters estimated.Taliban sees the Islamic State as an existential threat and has fought the group in Afghanistan for years.

Many Taliban militants defected to join the Islamic State affiliate, and the two groups fight for resources and territory.Their differences are also ideological, according to the Stanford center. Taliban has "compelling reasons" to target the Islamic State and could use newly acquired U.S.-made weapons to do so.

19

China's Game Plan in Afghanistan After The Taliban Take Over

The Taliban is inherently an inflexible, dogmatic and puritanical phenomenon that vehemently disallows exceptions, leniencies, and accommodations. For Beijing to genuinely believe that the Taliban in its new avatar will accede to Chinese interests (like Pakistan does), is very unlike and unbecoming of the perennially wary Chinese. The societal and political dynamics within Pakistan and Afghanistan are very different.

China is punting substantially on the return of the Taliban in Afghanistan, with a high-risk-high-return approach. While scenes of retreating US troops from Afghanistan may provide optical, rhetorical and political fodder to the Chinese to claim one upmanship in the stressed US-Sino equation, it also brings the extremist Taliban in direct control of the 91-kilometer land border between Afghanistan and China, at the Wakhan Corridor.

Hardnosed Chinese would recognise the practical risks involved in betting on the Taliban, but the potential $1 trillion worth of the world's largest lithium reserves in Afghanistan may make the risk worth a try. For now, the Chinese are displaying a gambler's sense and flexibility by insisting, 'some people stress their distrust for the Afghan Taliban ~ we want to say that nothing is unchanged forever'. This implies that the Chinese are willing to go against the obvious and bet on the Taliban.

The Taliban leaders are desperately looking for global recognition and ties with world powers, while China under Xi aims to exploit the war-ravaged country for its economic interests. Therefore, the China-Taliban relationship seems symbiotic. However, looking at the Taliban's past, the future of this new-found bonhomie looks bleak.

China was among the first countries to say it "stands ready" to work with the new Taliban regime, while in late July, China hosted a Taliban delegation committing economic cooperation. What will China's game plan be? Will Beijing remain cautious or step up its presence, particularly in the economic domain? What of China's long-standing concerns of the Taliban's links to Jihadist groups, including those blamed for attacks in China's Xinjiang region, which borders Afghanistan. Will the new situation in Afghanistan see a deepening China-Pakistan nexus, and what will be the implications for India.

Some analysts allege the treatment of Muslim minorities in China has strengthened the hand of Uyghur militants, who view China as an oppressor. Militants have sought a haven in the Afghanistan-Pakistan border regions for years, and China has reportedly attempted to negotiate with local parties in both countries to deprive them of that refuge. China however says its main aim in reaching out to the Taliban is to protect its western Xinjiang region from anti-Beijing East Turkestan Islamic Movement (ETIM) militants, who could seek sanctuary within Afghanistan.

The Afghanistan situation has literally forced China to adopt a proactive stance and dirty its hands, more even than it usually does in cross-border dissonances, and so overtly. Seeking to fill the void of a dominating 'foreign power' in Afghanistan has been a costly mistake since time immemorial. Yet the Chinese are betting on Taliban (willfully or circumstantially) in an extremely risky maneouver that could go terribly wrong for them.

China has dangled the prospect of providing the two things the Taliban needs to govern Afghanistan: diplomatic recognition and much-needed infrastructure and economic assistance. China is certain to exploit the new opening to make strategic inroads into mineral-rich Afghanistan and deepen its penetration of Pakistan, Iran, and Central Asia.

One of the initial projects could be the China-Afghanistan Economic Corridor, branching off from the CPEC at Pakistan Administered Kashmir and entering Afghanistan to be further extended to Iran and finally, the Chabahar port. This project would be useful in serving two agendas. The first would be to remove the Indian footprint in Chabahar port, and second to create assets worth billions of dollars which would facilitate Chinese industry, utilising Chinese finance to exploit Afghanistan's precious mineral resources relegating the country to a mere market meant for dumping Chinese goods.

China, in due course, would start offering loans to Afghanistan, initially at low, and later at market rates for building White Elephant-like projects, which would be grand in nature, but won't generate any revenue for Afghanistan as a country. Through these mechanisms, Afghanistan would be pushed into Chinese economic and thereafter political and strategic grip, just like other countries affected by the BRI such as Sri Lanka, Myanmar etc.

Pakistan is openly gloating over the Taliban "victory".

It may be upbeat but blowback in the form of Islamist terrorism and its economic fallout could be game changers. Afghanistan is bankrupt and foreign aid, which constituted around 60 per cent of its annual budget, has dried up. Pakistan is in no position to help it financially, which leaves only China with the capacity to fund it. But China does not dole out money for nothing. Will it provide financing in return for Afghanistan's mineral riches.

The analysts said, however, Islamabad's influence has waned over the years and Pakistan would likely be on guard over potential violence on its borders. Reports said the Taliban's return in Afghanistan could potentially embolden terror groups in Pakistan, including the Pakistani Taliban, which could affect the country's security.

20

India's Strategic Options in Afghanistan After Taliban Take Over

Uncertainty continues to loom over Afghanistan after Talibans take over. India would need soon to firm up its strategy to deal with the new despensation in Kabul. Admittedly India has no easy options here given Pakistan's links with Taliban. It would also rue its relations with Iran.

The situation in Afghanistan has emerged as a challenge for India which along with alignment and realignment of global powers led country to rethink its strategy. While India is unlikely to jump the gun on officially recognising the Taliban, but engagement with the Taliban is not ruled out.

The debate about whether India should engage with taliban discreetly or in the open has shifted to whether India should recognise the Taliban. There is a widespread feeling that India once again backed the wrong horse or atleast didn't do course correction and engage the Taliban sufficiently in advance to protect its interests. Some even recommend that India should recognise Taliban and be pragmatic since India is on weak ground and has very few options.

Although the argument for engagement or recognition as a way to limit our losses sounds good in the standard precepts of diplomacy. But it has to be tested against ground realities since some of Taliban leaders still work under Pakistan control. Also by recognising Taliban we will in effect be legitimising a Pakistani proxy terrorist conglomerate including the Haqqani network and rewarding the ISI.

India should not follow blindly the international community who are willing to be fooled by Pakistan to settle for a fig leaf of an inclusive government without real power. If at all there has to be an engagement to keep the people to people and trade relationship going it should be with minimal legitimization otherwise India should support the people from outside and facilitate that through Visas and other opportunities in India.

It is clear that even if one section of the taliban were to give India assurance of security, it will not be worth the paper it is signed on. There is also the ISI which will ensure that one of its several proxies sabotages any deal.

Good move would be for India to shore up its democratic credentials, to be more in sync with western democracies. Attracting censure for human rights and treatment for minorities will undermine the country's National interests .In the emerging global battle between autocracies and democracies, India must be firmly in the democracy camp.

India is not short of options, though none of ideal them are ideal. They range from complete or relative disengagement or non recognition to minimal engagement for practical needs without legitimizing them, to moral and diplomatic support for the resistance to the Taliban that has already begun.

Shunning a Taliban-dominated government may not be wise in the future, but the behaviour of the government in Kabul will be the defining factor, as will be Pakistan's behaviour. India will have to reopen the embassy in Kabul, as any prolonged absence on the ground will be detrimental to its interests.

New Delhi do not expect a peace deal, however. They view the Taliban as committed to its narrow and repressive interpretation of Islam and dominance of Afghan society. If the Taliban's bloody onslaught continues all the way to Kabul, it will spell the end of large-scale international aid, including from India.Delhi cannot shun a Taliban-dominated government. It will have to fine tune its diplomacy, engage China, Russia, Turkey and the US.

The Taliban is trying to project a reformed image, but its soldiers are reported to be conducting revenge killings and hunting down Afghans and foreigners who have worked for the Americans and the government.For India, this is a strategic setback, and raises the spectre of a revival of jihadi terrorism. Both China and Russia have been wary of terrorism spilling over into Xinjiang and Central Asia respectively. Both have refused to accept any refugees.Not only has the Taliban, traditionally an anti-India group, seized power, but India's Chinese and Pakistani rivals are now poised to deepen their footprints in Afghanistan.

India has had a stable relationship with the civilian Afghan government over the last two decades, providing the latter with development assistance. The shift in power has left New Delhi in a "tough strategic state". New Delhi has decided to wait and watch and keep a hawk's eye on the emerging situation. One option for India is to go along with the friends and allies in the region and the world in general, before beginning to deal with the Taliban as a recognised government.

India is especially worried because the last time the Taliban were in power, they sheltered pro-Pakistani militants, the analysts said. New Delhi is concerned that an emboldened Pakistan will use this as an opportunity to hit India; doing so would raise the potential of a broader India-Pakistan conflict.

21

How Potent is The Latest Threat By Al Qaeda To Kashmir ?

Al-Qaeda, the terror organization that masterminded the 9/11 attacks on the United States, has congratulated the Taliban and called for the "liberation of Kashmir".

The Taliban's return to power in Afghanistan has raised alarm in India that terrorist groups will rise up to threaten Kashmir, where New Delhi is locked in a decades long territorial dispute with neighbor Pakistan.

This is a new world. The terror threat has metastasized across the world, well beyond Afghanistan. The Taliban's resurgence in Afghanistan, historically called the "Heart of Asia" for its central location, has far-reaching implications for regional security, potentially including the simmering Kashmir dispute. The scenario New Delhi fears most is the Taliban's victory emboldening terrorist organizations in neighboring Pakistan, endangering Indian-controlled Kashmir. The events in Afghanistan have created a buzz in the Valley, with a section eyeing it as a victory for Islamic forces. For terrorist outfits too, it is being touted as a morale booster.

Terror launchpads close to the border are active again and infiltration has picked up, with agencies warning that this could point to an attempt by Pakistan to use the developments in Afghanistan to its advantage. Pakistan-based terrorist outfits Jaish-e-Mohammad and Lashkar-e-Taiba have stepped up efforts to push cadres into Jammu and Kashmir taking advantage of the shift in international focus on Afghanistan and a buzz over "victories" of Islamist forces, according to sources in the security establishment.

While there are fears that the Taliban takeover of Afghanistan may impact the security situation in the Kashmir Valley, there are also apprehensions that this could escalate terror-related violence in the Union Territory. However, the security officials in the field say that there is little chance of Taliban infiltrating into Kashmir as there is robust anti-infiltration grid at Line of Control (LoC).

People who have been alienated from the recent developments in Jammu and Kashmir including the historical abrogation of Article 370 seem to be almost joyous in anticipation of Taliban fighters marching towards Kashmir Valley. There could be a weapon upgrade with the Pakistan Army and terrorist groups getting their hands on huge supplies of weapons including stinger missiles captured by the Taliban from the Afghan National Army which surrendered recently.

But our security agencies sound confident for the challenges posed by the Taliban and Pakistan militant outfits supported by the Taliban. The situation is not the same as it was 20 years ago for the Taliban. But Indian Army has also honed its skills. Our personnel are well-trained and well-equipped for the situation. There is also border fence.

It is not that we are not ruling out possibility of handful of Taliban infiltrating. They will be tackled the same way as Pakistani terrorists.

According to intelligence inputs, Pakistan's intelligence agency Inter-Services Intelligence (ISI), in collaboration with terrorist organisations, is planning an attack in Jammu and Kashmir. Eight new routes have been fixed by Pakistan to send terrorists into India while a control room has been set up in Pakistan Occupied Kashmir (PoK), sources said. Intelligence input indicate that Pakistan has prepared 27 new launch pads near the line of control for infiltration in Jammu and Kashmir also these eight routes of infiltration are known to our intelligence agencies and security forces through various intercepts.

Qaeda statement is still being analysed, but it is a serious cause for concern for India. Al Qaeda is trying to radicalise Muslims in the world - it is dangerous for humanity. Pakistan is pushing ahead its agenda. It is intriguing that Kashmir was included in the statement as it was never on the agenda of the Taliban earlier. The Pakistan ISI is behind this statement of Qaeda. The omission of Chechnya in Russia and China's Xinjiang among targets of "liberation" through jihad is significant and telling.

Even though the Taliban never showed clear interest in Kashmir and has been reassuring the world that it has changed its tactics, the fact is that it has allowed many terror groups, including the Harkat-ul Ansar - an amalgamation of Harkat-ul-Mujahideen and Harkat-ul-Jihad-al-Islami - to use Afghan soil for pushing terrorists into Kashmir. Pakistan has been using Afghan soil to launch and train terrorists, so we have to be aware of new dynamics unfolding each passing minute.

For India, this is a strategic setback, and raises the

spectre of a revival of jihadi terrorism. Both China and Russia have been wary of terrorism spilling over into Xinjiang and Central Asia respectively. Both have refused to accept any refugees.

As regards the threat from ISIS to Kashmir, I feel it is not alarming since IS-K is rival of Taliban, US and and doesn't go well with Pak ISI. IS- K on the face of it and as part of the central design is against the governments of both The Taliban and Pakistan, however strategic and tactical opportunism by local actors and regional States has made IS-k much more difficult to follow its laid down policies.

In India, pro-ISIS individuals generally consider the Kashmir conflict as being geographic a fight over land by nationalists and patriots and not necessarily in the name of Islam. Such view could be altered as IS-K gains a foothold in Afghanistan, and spills over in Pakistan, Kashmir, and beyond: the ideological landscape could shift beyond just the Kashmir issue and become an all-encompassing cause of deeper sectarian fissures.

It is abundantly clear now that new interim government in Afghanistan has the strong imprint of Pakistan military jihadi complex. Pakistani backed factions have cornered all positions including Pro ISI Haqqani network. It is time for India to wait and watch yet be strongly prepared to thwart any infiltration designs by anyone.

Pakistan is openly gloating over the Taliban "victory". It may be upbeat but blowback in the form of Islamist terrorism and its economic fallout could be game changers. Afghanistan is bankrupt and foreign aid, which constituted around 60 per cent of its annual budget, has dried up. Pakistan is in no position to help it financially, which leaves only China with the capacity to fund it. But China does not dole out money for nothing. It will provide financing in return for Afghanistan's mineral riches.

The analysts said, however, Islamabad's influence has waned over the years and Pakistan would likely be on guard over potential violence on its borders. Reports said the Taliban's return in Afghanistan could potentially embolden terror groups in Pakistan, including the Pakistani Taliban, which could affect the country's security.

22

Despondency Looms Large Over New Taliban Government in Afghanistan (Its Economy is shattered)

A new Taliban interim government drawn exclusively from loyalist ranks formally begin work with the established headliners in all the key positions, with much grinding of teeth by the international community for the terrorists called extremists seizing reign of power in Kabul. Couple of foreign countries greeted the makeup of the new government in Afghanistan with caution and dismay after Taliban appointed hardliner veterans figures to top positions.

It is abundantly clear that Taliban new interim government in Afghanistan has the strong imprint of Pakistan military jihadi complex. The new Afghan leadership structure is sans non -Taliban members. Many old timers have found a place in the government as a reward for their role during the 20 years war. For Taliban it did not matter if the international community had put these leaders under travel and financial sanctions. Though Taliban had made lot of noises all through the Doha agreement negotiations about creating an inclusive government but when the government is finally announced it is anything but inclusive. People like Haqqani have been given powerful position whereas Mr Abdul Ghani Barather has been relegated to deputy prime ministers roll.

There are no Hazaras, just two Tajiks, one Uzbek and hardly any representation from the north in the government. Pashtuns from Southern part of Afghanistan, Talibans strong base have very less representation.

Given the lopsided composition of this government, protests from many sections of society are likely to continue. Of course there are no women included in the government.

All Punditry about the new Taliban was an exercise in desperate optimism. This makes international recognition for new Taliban regime difficult.

It's important to note that while some Taliban representatives say the group will be more conciliatory now than in the past and will abide by certain international norms, the group itself is not a monolith; rather, it's composed of numerous factions with varying degrees of extremism and propensity to support other terrorist groups. Foreseeable future, Afghanistan will be led by senior Taliban leaders who include in many cases the worst of the worst. Specifically to members of the Haqqani network, known as the most brutal faction of the Taliban.

The Taliban in Afghanistan have named a new interim government led by hardliners as the group pledges to implement a strict Islamic rule over the country of roughly 40 million. The new cabinet of the freshly restored Islamic Emirate of Afghanistan contains no women and no positions for opposition members or ethnic or religious minorities.

But the biggest challenge Taliban will face is in overcoming its economic crisis. US has frozen all Afghan reserves and World Bank and IMF have also stopped funding programs for Afghanistan. Pakistan for all its influence on Taliban can hardly financially prop up the new Kabul government given its own dire economic situation. Talibans only big hope is China who is interested in Afghanistan's rich mineral resources. But China is not likely to rush into unstable Afghanistan, since commercial exploitation of minerals which in lithium case can take up to 16 years. Unless Taliban government takes a pragmatic turn and negotiate with the west and India, it is looking at a humanitarian catastrophic. India should simply for now see how all this plays out in Afghanistan.

Now in the power vacuum created by US withdrawal from Afghanistan, China aims to dominate South Asia, first economically based on the China Pakistan economic corridor and then militarily using its alliance with Pakistan to establish military bases in Balochistan, this should be the critical link between Chinese military facilities and the South China sea and its naval base in Djibouti. Chinese navel and air bases in Balochistan would control the vital sea lanes of the Arabian sea.

China is first one to announce $ 31 million as aid to Afghanistan, its first after the Taliban seized power in Kabul as it backed the Afghan militant group's interim government saying it is a necessary step to restore order and end anarchy in Afghanistan.

Pakistan, not Afghanistan is the epicenter of Islamic militancy in South Asia using it to suppress ethnic separatism internally and as an instrument of its foreign policy, particularly against Afghanistan and India. The decline of terrorism in, J&K was not the consequence of any dearth of willing manpower or resources in Pakistan but of a very significant consolidation of Indian forces and declining popular support on the ground. It would be unwise now to dismiss all possibilities of escalation in the wake of Taliban return to power in Afghanistan, it will also be equally unwise to exaggerate the potential to arrive at some of the panic conclusions that are currently rife.

India should now give up all hopes that Taliban will be aggressive towards Pakistan once in power. This government it is without doubt, a Pakistan installed and Pakistan controlled administration. It means that any resumption of Indian diplomatic presence in Afghanistan will remain severely diminished for quite some time. Beyond limited contact to enable humanitarian assistance the risk of engaging with this administration far outweighs the benefits.

To say that Joe Biden has handed over the key to a rare resource — rare earth elements (REEs) — to the Taliban and, in turn, paved the way to Chinese supremacy in this crucial area, would seem like an overstatement. But it is true that the withdrawal of US troops in Afghanistan has opened the doors for the Chinese to extract resources.

The most dependable assessment is that the Kabul regime will be under pressure from four directions: Pakistan, for security and past links; China, for investment; Russia, for intelligence; and the US/EU, for the ability to conduct finance globally. So far, the Pakistan hand is showing up with prominence.

Afghanistan is rich in resources like copper, gold, oil, natural gas, uranium, bauxite, coal, iron ore, rare earths, lithium, chromium, lead, zinc, gemstones, talc, sulphur, travertine, gypsum and marble. Torn by four decades of war and desperate poverty, Afghanistan is believed to be sitting on one of the richest troves of minerals in the world. The value of these resources has been roughly estimated between $1-3 trillion. Illegal mining is rampant throughout Afghanistan, with more than 2,000 such sites raising money for warlords and the insurgency.

While much of the world has adopted a wait-and-see approach to engagement with the Taliban, China has already said it is ready to build friendly relations with the group following their takeover.

23

Will Taliban Bring 'Achhe Din' For Pakistan ?

Pakistan hopes that the new interim government in Afghanistan led by the Taliban would bring "peace, security and stability" to the war-torn country and work towards taking care of humanitarian and development needs of the Afghan people. The Taliban takeover in Afghanistan has delivered a strategic victory to Pakistan establishing a friendly government in Kabul for the first time in nearly 20 years but Pakistan may soon find that friendship with Taliban won't come quite so easily.

Pakistan, which celebrated Taliban takeover of Afghanistan is now waking up to the realisation that the group's victory is inciting terrorists into insurgency in its own region, according to media reports. When Pakistan Prime Minister Imran Khan applauded the Taliban's victory and said that they broke "shackles of slavery", he was unaware that the outfit's victory in a neighbouring country can trigger militants in his own.

Another beneficiary of the collapse of the Afghan

government is likely to be the Pakistan Taliban who have been at war with the Pakistani army for years. The Afghan Taliban have a murky relationship with their Pakistani counterpart. Certainly, individuals in the Afghan Taliban are in touch with their Pakistani fellow believers and will offer safe haven in their new conquests. There may be a serious blowback in time. Pakistani officials are also afraid that Tehreek-i-Taliban Pakistan (Pakistani Taliban) could resurface in the wake of the Taliban's victory in the neighbouring country as TTP is allied to the Afghan Taliban. Experts have also said that the Taliban's victory has added a volatile element to the mainstream politics playing out on Pakistan's streets.

Now, Islamabad is noticing the unrest washing across the Afghan border. After the recent victory of the Taliban, the militant groups are incited to create an insurgency in Pakistan. Taliban, not only inspired the militants but also Pakistan's hard-line religious parties that aim to reshape the country in a more fundamentalist Islamist image. The Afghan Taliban are virulently anti-Shiite. There have already been incidents of violence. That will increase sectarian tension in Pakistan which has a much larger Shiite population than Afghanistan.

As neighboring Afghanistan plunges further into conflict, Pakistani officials fear fighting and refugees will surge across the border. There are large number of refugees gathered on all xing places on Afghan- Pak border ie Chaman, Torkham and Spin Boldak, but they are not permitted to enter Pak, since there are already large number crossed over. But how long? The Durand line divides Pashtuns of the region into two countries and creates territorial disputes mainly in Khyber Pakhtunkhwa and Balochistan. Theconsolidation of the southern Taliban in Afghanistan could reignite the fire of nationalism in the region. Early indicators after the Taliban victory also do not suggest an end to Pakistan's Pashtunistan problem.

Interesting Taliban has released hundreds of TTP captives from Afghanistan jail who are now trying to unify all mujahid fections to realise the formation of an Emirate in Pakistan. With this China has a problem for security of their CPEC projects which are being severely objected by TTP and Balochistan Liberation Army.

The only hope Pakistan has with Taliban coming to power is to intensify trouble in Kashmir with the help of Haqqanis and Other terrorist groups, which is also not that easy as the security forces in India are fully geared to receive them.

Pakistan would continue to ride its most effective and time-tested strategies against India—using an array of militant groups as proxies to continuously bleed India. These groups that were operating in Afghanistan no longer have US troops to turn their gun, giving them the motivation to refocus their attention and pent-up energy on the Indian part of Kashmir.

India has got the ability to influence the calculus of Afghanistan. There is too much at stake and New Delhi should become more proactively involved and not be shy of even shoring up military engagement with Afghanistan.

When seen in the context of the the emerging great game, it is pretty clear that Islamabad and Rawalpindi's control over Taliban is neither durable nor entirely remote-controlled. Once the brief honeymoon gives way to sobering realities, Pakistan will likely have to get ready for another period of Tumult.

24

Likely Hurdles in Taliban's Governence of Afghanistan

Taliban is back is power in Afghanistan on the 20th anniversary of 9/11 is immensely painful to the United States, NATO, and many Afghans. In 2001, the U.S. overthrew the Taliban regime to defeat al-Qaida.

U.S. also sought to vanquish the Taliban and leave behind a pluralistic, human-rights-respecting, and economically - sustainable Afghan state. It failed in those objectives. There were plenty of mistakes and problems with the international efforts, but most importantly the United States never succeeded in inducing good governance in Afghanistan or persuading Pakistan to stop its multifaceted support for the Taliban.

The Taliban have won the war now they have to govern Afghanistan. The transition presents an enormous test for the Islamists in a desperately poor, diplomatically isolated country where deep-seated political and social problems have been compounded by more than four decades of war. Will the Taliban be able to maintain itself in power?

The answer depends on how it handles and prevents armed opposition to its rule and manages the country's economy and relations with external actors.

The new regime should rule across just about all dimensions of governance: inclusiveness, dealing with foreign fighters, the economy, and external relations. Many middle-level battlefield commanders – younger, more plugged into global jihadi networks, and without personal experience of the Taliban's mismanaged 1990s rule – are more hardline than key older national and provincial leaders. If the Taliban rules very brutally, international actors will maintain sanctions on the group and perhaps intensify them.

The Taliban regime faces the loss of billions of dollars that had been allocated to Afghanistan from the International Monetary Fund, the World Bank, the U.S., and the European Union while the country's central bank reserves held in the U.S. were frozen by the U.S. government. Beyond immiserating already desperately poor people hit by COVID-19, drought, and economic contractions in a country where 90% of people live in poverty and 30% are acutely food insecure, such a ban would also eliminate income for Taliban middle-layer commanders and rank-and-file fighters.

Winning that war might just turn out to be the easy part, as maintaining peace and governing the conflict-wracked and impoverished country will be a tough nut to crack.This crunch could spell disaster, as the Taliban need to figure out how to pay government employees and keep running critical infrastructure such as water, power and communications. Significant mineral wealth remains underground as instability has prevented major exploration and international investment. The Taliban cannot simply double its poppy economy, the global market is already saturated with opioids.

It would also need humanitarian agencies to provide

urgent aid to Afghans displaced by the war. More than 5 million Afghans are estimated to be internally displaced. The UN says nearly 400,000 people have been displaced this year alone as a result of ongoing violence. Government employees are facing financial problems in Afghanistan as government offices have mostly remained closed since the Ashraf Ghani government collapsed.

The Taliban will struggle to find jobs for the many now-unemployed soldiers of the Afghan security forces whom the United States paid. Even if half of the nominal force were "ghost soldiers" or are dead and, say, only 150,000 soldiers actually fought, they are now a loose force without income for themselves and their families. They melted before the Taliban; but in time they may resort to banditry or be tempted to join old or new militias, if only to get economic rents.

As US-led forces began to withdraw and the previous government started to lose control, Afghans with skills, experience and resources headed for the exits. They included bureaucrats, bankers, doctors, engineers, professors and university graduates, all terrified of life under the Islamists. The Taliban appear aware of the impact such a brain drain could have on the Afghan economy.

It needs technocrats and foreign assistance, both advisory and on the ground, such as in the form of humanitarian NGOs. If its rule centers on purges and revenge, of which distressing reports have emerged, the technocrats will continue to flee. The Taliban can only pressure them so much to work under duress. It has no experience with or technocratic capacity for delivering or even just maintaining other existing services such as electricity or water delivery, let alone tackling complex issues like setting macroeconomic policies.

The Taliban are a predominantly Pashtun, Islamic

fundamentalist group that returned to power in Afghanistan in 2021 after waging a twenty-year insurgency. The Taliban may have taken control of Afghanistan but the threat of terror attacks in the country has not ended with their insurgency.

The Taliban and IS are both hardline Sunni extremists, but the latter has an even harsher and brutal interpretation of Islamic law. IS has said it will continue to fight in Afghanistan, and its statements have described the Taliban as apostates. Possible defections of Taliban factions or foreign fighters in Afghanistan could boost the Taliban's principal rival, the Islamic State Khorasan (ISK), whom the Taliban has battled for years. The IS-K cannot currently bring the Taliban regime down. But it could become an envelope for any future defections.

Since regaining control, the Taliban have taken actions reminiscent of their brutal rule in the late 1990s. They have cracked down on protesters, reportedly detained and beaten journalists, and reestablished their Ministry for the Promotion of Virtue and Prevention of Vice, which under previous Taliban rule enforced prohibitions on behavior deemed un-Islamic. The group's acting higher education minister said women will be permitted to study at universities in gender-segregated classrooms and wearing Islamic attire.

West's bargaining and engagement with the Taliban should focus on specific demands, such as reducing the most debilitating repression, and center on discreet and specific punishments and inducements for concrete policy actions in what will be a long, complicated, iterative, and turbulent process.

If the Taliban does not prevent the leakage of anti-Shia terrorism into Iran from Taliban factions, foreign fighters, or ISK Iran could attempt to activate its Fatimiyoun units in Afghanistan. The Fatimiyoun are Afghan Shia fighters, numbering the tens of thousands, whom Iran trained and deployed to fight in Syria and Libya. Having returned to Afghanistan, they could battle the Taliban's rule.

Whether the Taliban can accommodate Tehran, Beijing, and Moscow's principal counterterrorism interests, which they judge far more important than any economic opportunities Afghanistan offers. If terrorism leakages are extensive, only Afghanistan's trade with Pakistan may survive.

These various challenges ahead do not mean that the West can easily topple the Taliban regime through sanctions or induce it to preserve the political pluralism and human and women's rights as they existed at least formally over the past 20 years.

Ashraf Ghani who is now cooling his heels in UAE will remember how he started his presidency on a decidedly different note by attempting a paradigm shift in the traditional Afghan outlook by trying to befriend Pakistan, he gave it the long rope, only to see the noose prepared by Islamabad around his own neck. Much before the Taliban entered Kabul, he fled ingloriously. The failed leader's hasty escape led to many accusing him of "betrayal" (apparently made worse with credible murmurs of four cars stashed with money), an ultimate shame and humiliation in the age-old code of honour amongst the proud Pashtuns, i.e., Pashtunwali.

The Taliban-led Afghanistan could be the latest entrant to the Chinese 'bloc' as the other 'bloc' of the 'Free World' would be morally bound to maintain a distance from the revisionist and extremist Taliban for whom, too, there is no practical alternative but to sew itself to the Chinese 'bloc' for sovereign legitimacy. The introductions and familiarisation of the boorish Taliban leadership can be ably handled by their progenitors i.e. the Pakistani 'establishment', which has deep access and relationship with the Afghan Taliban and the Chinese.

25

Is Panjshir Still Resuscitating in Afghanistan ?

The Panjshir valley, a rugged groove cut into the Hindu Kush mountains, has a storied reputation of resisting invasion. There are two main points of entry into the valley, both of which require passing through unforgiving terrain and complicated topography. Its towns are spread across the valley floor, surrounded by the icy blue waters of the Panjshir river and the daunting bare-ribbed mountains that tower above. Blending into the gorgeous scenery, the streets of Panjshir are littered with decaying tanks and machinery, remnants of the Soviet era that stand as a stark reminder of the region's violent past.

Panjshir is home to the largest population of ethnic Tajiks living in Afghanistan which shapes the region's political and cultural identity. Although they don't have strong ties to Tajikistan, their value system is markedly different from the country's dominant Pashtun population. The Taliban, a predominantly Pashtun organisation, has historically struggled to gain support in Panjshir despite recent attempts to include Tajiks within their ranks. Panjshir, due to its heavy supply of minerals, is also wealthier on average than the rest of Afghanistan and considers itself to be an almost autonomous region,

Panjshir fighters earned a legendary reputation for resistance, defending their mountain homes first from the Soviet military for a decade, then throughout a civil war, then the last Taliban regime from 1996 - 2001. Several Panjshir leaders, including Ahmad Massoud the son of the late veteran fighter Ahmad Shah Massoud, vowed never to surrender to the Taliban. Taliban were emboldened by their sweeping victories across the rest of the country, where they seized an enormous arsenal of weapons and military kit that the now-departed US provided to the defeated Afghan army.

The Taliban said their forces had fought their way into the provincial capital of Panjshir, the valley where opposition forces have been holding out since the fall of Kabul three weeks ago. The police headquarters and district centre of Rukhah, adjacent to the provincial capital Bazarak, had fallen, and opposition forces had suffered numerous casualties, with large numbers of prisoners and captured vehicles, weapons and ammunition.

Nearly two weeks after the Taliban celebrated victory in the holdout province of Panjshir, parts of the rugged valley lie empty and abandoned, populated by only old men and livestock. Despite credible reports that suggest the NRF is still active, its ability to drive the Taliban out of the Panjshir valley is likely limited. The group suffers from a lack of internal leadership and more significantly, external support.

In this lush strip of land walled off from potential invaders by high mountain peaks and narrow, ambush-prone passes former mujahedeen fighters and Afghan commandos regrouped in the days after the Taliban toppled the Afghan government, vowing to fight to the last man. With its history of resistance and its reputation for impenetrability, the Panjshir Valley seemed an ideal place for a determined force of renegades to base an insurgency.

By Sept. 6, however, the Taliban claimed to have captured the entire province of Panjshir, a momentous victory in a region that repelled numerous Soviet offensives in the 1980s, and had remained beyond the Taliban's control during its rule from 1996 to 2001. During those weeks of fighting and even after, reports of the Taliban committing human rights abuses against captured resistance fighters and civilians circulated on social media. Yet the accounts of door-to-door search and seizures as well as public executions, all of which the Taliban denied, were impossible to verify or debunk.

Electricity and cellphone towers were cut, leaving an information vacuum that quickly filled with opposing narratives and claims of massacres, ethnic cleansing and false charges. A widely shared video claiming Pakistani drones were operating over the valley turned out to be graphics from a video game.

The fall of the Panjshir Valley to the Taliban forces did not draw an immediate response from India. Taliban forces conquered the strategically important region amidst reports that the leader of the resistance fighters Ahmad Massoud has left for a secure place outside Afghanistan. Analysts here maintain that the situation in Afghanistan is unlikely to stabilise because of multiple internal and external factors.

Pictures on social media showed Taliban members standing in front of the gate of the Panjshir provincial governor's compound after fighting over the weekend with the National Resistance Front of Afghanistan (NRFA), led by Panjshiri leader Ahmad Massoud. The Taliban assured the people of Panjshir, who are ethnically distinct from the

Pashtun-dominated Taliban and fought against the Islamists during their 1996 - 2001 rule, that there would be no "discriminatory act against them".

Panjshir was the last pocket of armed resistance against the Taliban. It has a history of being difficult for enemies to take. The rugged mountain valley is still littered with the wreckage of tanks destroyed during the long war against the Soviet Union in the 1980s.

The Panjshir Resistance may have folded up for now after its leaders, Amrullah Saleh and Ahmad Massoud have left Afghanistan, according to sources here. While Saleh is said to be in Tajikistan, Massoud is in a European country, believed to be France.

Sources said the withdrawal of leading members of the National Resistance Front (NRF) from the fray shows the unwillingness of any other country to provide a rear base for the Panjshir militants. The NRF also could not succeed in extending its resistance outside the confines of the Valley except for a couple of neighbouring districts with majority Tajik populations.

Unlike in the 1990s, when the Northern Alliance were able to control the supply lines from Tajikistan to the Panjshir valley, this time the Taliban captured the provinces to the north of Panjshir. As a result, they were able to surround the valley, and to effectively cut off supply lines of arms, ammunition, fighters, food, and fuel to the resistance.

Pakistan helped the Taliban with arms, ammunition and, reports suggest, even fighter jets to outmanoeuvre the opposition.Themobilisation of Pakistani air assets was a game changer that created asymmetry between the Taliban and the forces of the Northern Alliance, and ultimately tilted the balance in the former's favour. The presence of the ISI chief in Kabul was indication of the key role that Rawalpindi played. Iran has criticised the Pakistani military for "foreign interference" in the affairs of Afghans.

The US and its allies abandoned the Northern Alliance completely. When Ahmad Shah Massoud, the legendary "Lion of Panjshir" and father of the young leader of the resistance Ahmad Massoud, was commander of the anti-Taliban forces, several among the international community had helped the Northern Alliance with men and material. Ahmad Shah Massoud was assassinated by al-Qaeda 20 years ago, just two days before the 9/11 attacks that shook the world and triggered the US-led war on terror.

26

Dilemma of Taliban in Formation of New Government

Alarm bells are ringing in various capitals following the appointment of ultraradicals and listed terrorists in the Taliban's new government in Afghanistan. One particular capital that feels rattled by this government formation is New Delhi, India. As many Western powers follow a wait-and-see policy, New Delhi is taking a proactive role in reaching out to like-minded friends to cobble together a narrative that is likely to be anti-Taliban and may lead to some heavy-handed approaches in dealing with this new regime.

There was little surprise in the Taliban's announcement of an all-male government composed almost entirely of its old guard and with top posts going to hardliners. It was nevertheless a disappointment and at odds with their earlier statements and assurances to the international community that they would form a broad-based government. The cabinet is anything but inclusive and hardly reflects the country's ethnic diversity. Almost half its members served in the Taliban's government in 1996-2001.

Taliban spokesmen described it as a 'caretaker' arrangement that kept open the door to later expansion by accommodating others. There is however little to suggest they will do this. It is at the start of their rule that the Taliban needed to demonstrate to their people and the world that they were willing to depart from the past. If they had included non-Taliban members from minorities and women, they may have been able to change the international conversation and perception of them.

Reminiscent of their previous harsh rule in the 1990s, the Taliban have already begun to wipe out some of Afghanistan's gains of 20 years. They've denied women a seat at the Cabinet, beaten journalists into silence and enforced their severe interpretation of Islam, on occasion violently.

The economic challenges are steep. Most Afghans live on less than $2 a day, 80% of the country's budget was covered by international funds over the past 20 years, and no industries of note have emerged to provide employment to a mostly young population. Tens of thousands of Afghans have fled, most of them members of the educated elite.

Yet despite such dependence on international support, the Taliban sent a message with their Cabinet lineup this week that they intend to run Afghanistan on their terms. They named a government filled with veterans of their 1990s rule and the subsequent insurgency against a U.S.-led military coalition. Their Cabinet includes former Guantanamo Bay prisoners and — perhaps one of the most eyebrow-raising appointments — Sirajuddin Haqqani, wanted by the FBI for questioning in several deadly attacks, as interior minister.

In portraying their Cabinet as a caretaker administration, the Taliban signaled there is still room for change and that other nations can do business with this government without recognizing it first.

Prolonged economic stagnation could lead to protests by the country's growing poor who might eventually decide they have little to lose by openly challenging the hard-line rulers. Afghans of 2021 are not the compliant population of 1996 — a time when the Taliban had little trouble imposing their uncompromising edicts.

But the opportunity was squandered. Flushed with victory Taliban leaders seemed to have followed their instincts rather than exercise prudence. They may also have mistaken engagement for acceptance by the international community. Engagement on practical issues is not endearment.

The international reaction to the new government has been circumspect including from Pakistan. Western countries have in fact responded sceptically with officials pointing out that this was not the promised inclusive government.

Taliban may have succeeded in eliminating armed resistance but that does not rule out public resistance down the road. After all this is not Afghanistan of the 1990s. Adept at fighting, the Taliban confront governance challenges fundamentally different from when they were last in power.

The fraught economic situation can spawn public discontent even unrest over time. With its foreign exchange reserves frozen by the US, assistance from the IMF/World Bank suspended and people facing food and cash shortages as well as rising prices the danger looms of a serious economic crisis. That should be reason enough to urge the Taliban government to show flexibility and be responsive to international expectations to secure the flow of funds to avert an economic collapse.

While foreign governments and aid groups evacuate thousands of people, they're leaving billions of dollars in projects hanging in the balance, much of it through the Afghanistan Reconstruction Trust Fund.

New Delhi successfully used Afghanistan to isolate its regional rival Pakistan. India leveraged is position with the Western-backed regime in Kabul by implementing several large-scale soft-power undertakings in the country with a view to extracting long-term benefits.

Now the tables have turned, once again, for New Delhi. Owing to India's intimate links to the previous civilian regime in Afghanistan, the Taliban view the former with a healthy dose of suspicion.

Also concern are growing at the increased constraints the Taliban government has placed on the news media in Afghanistan, their new rules open the door for censorship and repression.

In one of the most symbolic moments since the takeover of Kabul on August 15, the militants paraded on Wednesday some of the military hardware they had captured during their offensive, even flying a Black Hawk helicopter over Kandahar, their movement's spiritual heartland.

Now, all eyes are on whether the Taliban can deliver a Cabinet capable of managing a war-wracked economy and honour the movement's pledges of a more "inclusive" government.

In the western city of Herat, some 50 women took to the streets in a rare, defiant protest for the right to work and over the lack of women's participation in the new government.

Herat is a relatively cosmopolitan city on the ancient silk road near the Iranian border. It is one of the more prosperous in Afghanistan and girls have already returned to school there.

Also concern are growing at the increased constraints the Taliban government has placed on the news media in Afghanistan, their new rules open the door for censorship and repression.

Index

Abdul Ghani
------ Alipoor 44
------ Barather 103
Abdul Rashid Dostum 73
Abu Musab 64
Afghan
------ forces and Taliban 68
------ Armed Forces 57
------ army soldiers 82
------ government 69, 70, 71
------ Mujahedeen 23
------ National Army 87, 98
------ national government 58
------ peace process 28
------ refugee 11, 28
------ society 8, 71, 95
------ Taliban 74, 82, 90, 108
------ tribals 15
------ - Pak border 108
Afghanistan 7, 14, 32, 36, 41
------ economy 80
------ Reconstruction Trust Fund 122
------ -Pakistan border 90
Afghanistan's military history 81
Ahmad Massoud 116, 117, 118
Ahmad Shah Massoud 82, 119
Al-Qaeda 36, 97
------ and ISIS 20
------ movement 20
Al-Shabab 22
all-covering burka 18
'all-weather friend' 23, 61
Amrullah Saleh 45, 118
anti-Shia terrorism 113
anti-Taliban forces 82
Article 370 98
Ashraf Ghani 49, 114
------ government 8, 25, 112
Atta Mohammad Noor 73

Bagram Air Base 37

Balochistan Liberation Army 109
Bamiyan Buddha statues 18
Baradar 62
Belt and Road Initiative 31, 34, 51, 54, 61, 77
Benazir Bhutto 44
Bill Clinton administration 57
Blinken proposal 29

'caretaker' 121
Chaotic collapse 73
China 31, 79, 91, 104
------ abhors 53
------ and Russia 54
------ and Tajikistan 82
------ Pakistan Economic Corridor 61
------ under Xi 90
-------Afghanistan Economic Corridor 91
-------Pakistan nexus 90
-------Taliban relationship 90
China's new friend 60
CPEC 24, 29
------ projects 109

DAB's foreign currency 79
Doha 65
------ Accord 29
------ agreement 102
Doha Peace Accord 8, 52
Durand Lines 28

East Turkistan Islamic Movement 23, 53, 61, 62, 79, 90
economic challenges 121
economic interests 79
"exchange of suitcases" 44

Financial Action Task Force 59
financial problems in Afghanistan 112
first Afghan war 39
'Friendship Gate' 45
fundamentalist Taliban 52

"Graveyard of Empires" 11, 13, 25, 36
Guantanamo Bay prisoners 121
guerrilla movement 83

Hakimullah Mehsud 18
Hamdullah Mohib 25
Hamid Karzai 49
Haqqani network 94, 103
Harkat-ul Ansar 99
Harkat-ul-Jihad-al-Islami 99
Harkat-ul-Mujahideen 99
"Heart of Asia" 97
historical Battlefield 7

illegal drug trade 56
Imran Khan 27, 107
India 95

India-Pakistan conflict 96
Indian interests in Afghanistan 76
India's influence in Afghanistan 56
insurgency in Kashmir 86
intra-Afghan negotiations 56
intra-Afghan talks 29, 57
Iraq and Syria 73
IS- K 100
ISI 9, 19, 86, 94, 99
ISIS 100
ISIS in Afghanistan 85
ISIS-K 21, 84, 88
"Islamic emirate" 8, 14, 42
Islamic terrorism 87
Islamist Dogma on Afghanistan 8
Islamists extremists in Afghanistan 8, 76
Ismail Khan 48, 73
issue of Kashmir 86

Jaise-e-Mohammad 86
----- and Lashkar-e-Taiba 98
Jihadhism 78
Jihadies 56
Joe Biden 15, 105

Kabul 7
Khorasan 14

land of the Afghans 13
Lashkar-e-Jhangvi 44
Lashkar- e- Taiba 86
----- and Lashkar-e-Jahangvi 87
----- and Jaish-e-Mohamed 29
"liberation of Kashmir" 97
"Lion of Panjshir" 82, 119
Long War Journal 40

madrassas in Pakistan 18
Malala Yousafzai 18
Massoud and his United Front 82
Maulawi Hibatullah Akhundzada 20
Metallurgical Corporation of Chin 33
Michni Point 15
mineral-rich Afghanistan 91
"minority" status in Afghanistan 44
"moribund" 42
mujahedeen fighters 116
Mullah Mansour 20
Mullah Mohammad Omar 9, 20
Muslim minorities in China 90

Najeeb Ulla 55
National Resistance Front 117, 118
NATO 26

new Afghan regime 80
New Taliban interim government 9
new Taliban rulers 20
non-Pashtun insurgency 80
North Atlantic Treaty Organization forces 47

Pakistan and Afghanistan 9
Pakistan and China 48
Pakistan Taliban 108
Pakistan-based terrorist 98
Pakistan-sponsored terrorism 57
Pakistani 'double game 54
Pakistani military-jihadi complex 56, 74, 87
Pakistani proxy terrorist 94
Pakistani Taliban 61, 78
-------- attacks 18
Panjshir 116, 118
Panjshir fighters 116
Panjshir River 81
Panjshir Valley 81, 82, 83, 115
Panjwai 49
Pashtun movement 17
Pashtun-led Taliban 78
"peace agreement" 22
Peace in Afghanistan 58
"peace, security and stability" 107
'peace-dialogue 38
PoK 87, 99
President Ashraf Ghani 43
President Burhanuddin Rabbani 17
President Joe Biden 22, 26, 37

Qaeda statement 99
Qasem Soleimani 67
Quetta Shura" 19

sanctuary in Afghanistan 85
Second World War 37
"shackles of slavery" 10
Shah Mahmood Qureshi 28
Sheikh Rashid Ahmed 55
Shiite Iran 53
Sirajuddin Haqqani 121
Soviet-Afghan war 23
stopped funding programs 104
'strategic engagement' 25
strong comeback in Afghanistan 86
Sunni Muslim insurgent group 48
Sunni-supremacist Taliban 53

Tajik ethnic group 81
Taliban 18, 42, 50, 57, 73, 75, 76, 84, 89, 93, 110, 121, 122
------ and IS 113
------ and Pakistan 100
------ attacked Kandhar 56

------ fighters 70, 98
------ in Afghanistan 10, 19, 89, 103
------ leadership 55
------ march 44
------ movement 47
------ new interim government in Afghanistan 102
------ regime in Afghanistan 29
------ takeover in Afghanistan 107
------ victory in Afghanistan 75
------- Al Qaida groups 23
-------dominated government 95
-------free area 83
-------led Afghanistan 114
-------run Afghanistan 27, 38
------/ISI victory in Afghanistan 9
Talibans 77
Taliban's
------ government in 1996-2001 120
------ return to power in Afghanistan 97
------ rule in Afghanistan 78
------ takeover of Afghanistan 38, 79
Tehreek-e-Labbaik 45
Tehrik-i-Taliban 41, 48, 108
'terrorist activities' in Afghanistan 38
the great game 7
Trade Center attacks 20
Turkestan Islamic Party 23

Uighur uprising 38
US
------ and Russia 34
------ Taliban agreement 56
------ Threat Assessment Report 39
------ troops in Afghanistan 105
------ war in Afghanistan 22
------ withdrawal 31, 104
US-Taliban peace talks 24
Uyghur militants 53, 90
Uyghurs of China 87

Vice President Amrullah Saleh 81

Wakhan Corridor 89
"war on terror" 78
withdrawal of NATO 7
withdrawal of Soviet troops 9

Xinjiang and Central Asia 95

zero-tolerance policy 74